AMERICAN POETRY
1922

A MISCELLANY

**Edited By
LOUIS UNTERMEYER**

Granger Poetry Library

GRANGER BOOK CO., INC.
Great Neck, N.Y.

FIRST PUBLISHED 1922
REPRINTED 1976

ISBN 0-89609-052-3

PRINTED IN THE UNITED STATES OF AMERICA

A FOREWORD

WHEN the first Miscellany of American Poetry appeared in 1920, innumerable were the questions asked by both readers and reviewers of publishers and contributors alike. The modest note on the jacket appeared to satisfy no one. The volume purported to have no editor, yet a collection without an editor was pronounced preposterous. It was obviously not the organ of a school, yet it did not seem to have been compiled to exploit any particular phase of American life; neither Nature, Love, Patriotism, Propaganda, nor Philosophy could be acclaimed as its reason for being, and it was certainly not intended, as has been so frequent of late, to bring a cheerful absence of mind to the world-weary during an unoccupied ten minutes. Again, it was exclusive not inclusive, since its object was, evidently, not the meritorious if impossible one of attempting to be a compendium of present-day American verse.

But the publisher's note had stated one thing quite clearly, that the Miscellany was to be a biennial. Two years have passed, and with the second volume it has seemed best to state at once the reasons which actuated its contributors to join in such a venture.

A Foreword

In the first place, the plan of the *Miscellany* is frankly imitative. For some years now there has been published in England an anthology entitled Georgian Poetry. The Miscellany is intended to be an American companion to that publication. The dissimilarities of temperament, range and choice of subjects are manifest, but the outstanding difference is this: *Georgian Poetry* has an editor, and the poems it contains may be taken as that editor's re-action to the poetry of the day. The *Miscellany,* on the other hand, has no editor; it is no one person's choice which forms it; it is not an attempt to throw into relief any particular group or stress any particular tendency. It does disclose the most recent work of certain representative figures in contemporary American literature. The poets who appear here have come together by mutual accord and, although they may invite others to join them in subsequent volumes as circumstance dictates, each one stands (as all newcomers also must stand) as the exponent of fresh and strikingly diverse qualities in our native poetry. It is as if a dozen unacademic painters, separated by temperament and distance, were to arrange to have an exhibition every two years of their latest work. They would not pretend that they were the only painters worthy of a public showing; they would maintain that their work was, generally speaking, most interesting to one another. Their gallery would necessarily be limited; but it would be flexible enough to admit, with every fresh exhibit, three or

iv

four new members who had achieved an importance and an idiom of their own. This is just what the original contributors to the *Miscellany* have done.

The newcomers—H. D., Alfred Kreymborg, and Edna St. Vincent Millay—have taken their places with the same absence of judge or jury that marks any " society of independents." There is no hanging committee; no organizer of " position." Two years ago the alphabet determined the arrangement; this time seniority has been the sole arbiter of precedence. Furthermore—and this can not be too often repeated—there has been no editor. To be painstakingly precise, each contributor has been his own editor. As such, he has chosen his own selections and determined the order in which they are to be printed, but he has had no authority over either the choice or grouping of his fellow exhibitors' contributions. To one of the members has been delegated the merely mechanical labors of assembling, proof-reading, and seeing the volume through the press. The absence of E. A. Robinson from this year's *Miscellany* is a source of regret not only to all the contributors but to the poet himself. Mr. Robinson has written nothing since his Collected Poems with the exception of a long poem—a volume in itself—but he hopes to appear in any subsequent collection.

It should be added that this is not a haphazard anthology of picked-over poetry. The poems that follow are new. They are new not only in the sense that (with two exceptions) they cannot be found in book form, but most of them have never previously been published. Certain of the selections have appeared in recent magazines and these are reprinted by permission of *The Century, The Yale Review, Poetry: A Magazine of Verse, The New Republic, Harper's, Scribner's, The Bookman, The Freeman, Broom, The Dial, The Atlantic Monthly, Farm and Fireside, The Measure,* and *The Literary Review.* Vachel Lindsay's " I Know All This When Gipsy Fiddles Cry " is a revised version of the poem of that name which was printed in *The Enchanted Years.*

CONTENTS

Contents

Contents

Contents

AMY LOWELL

Amy Lowell

LILACS

Lilacs,
False blue,
White,
Purple,
Color of lilac,
Your great puffs of flowers
Are everywhere in this my New England.
Among your heart-shaped leaves
Orange orioles hop like music-box birds and sing
Their little weak soft songs;
In the crooks of your branches
The bright eyes of song sparrows sitting on spotted
      eggs
Peer restlessly through the light and shadow
Of all Springs.
Lilacs in dooryards
Holding quiet conversations with an early moon;
Lilacs watching a deserted house
Settling sideways into the grass of an old road;
Lilacs, wind-beaten, staggering under a lopsided
      shock of bloom
Above a cellar dug into a hill.
You are everywhere.
You were everywhere.
You tapped the window when the preacher preached
      his sermon,
And ran along the road beside the boy going to
      school.

Amy Lowell

You stood by pasture-bars to give the cows good
     milking,
You persuaded the housewife that her dish-pan was
     of silver
And her husband an image of pure gold.
You flaunted the fragrance of your blossoms
Through the wide doors of Custom Houses—
You, and sandal-wood, and tea,
Charging the noses of quill-driving clerks
When a ship was in from China.
You called to them: " Goose-quill men, goose-quill
     men,
May is a month for flitting,"
Until they writhed on their high stools
And wrote poetry on their letter-sheets behind the
     propped-up ledgers.
Paradoxical New England clerks,
Writing inventories in ledgers, reading the " Song of
     Solomon " at night,
So many verses before bedtime,
Because it was the Bible.
The dead fed you
Amid the slant stones of graveyards.
Pale ghosts who planted you
Came in the night time
And let their thin hair blow through your clustered
     stems.
You are of the green sea,
And of the stone hills which reach a long dis-
     tance.

4

Amy Lowell

You are of elm-shaded streets with little shops where
      they sell kites and marbles,
You are of great parks where every one walks and
      nobody is at home.
You cover the blind sides of greenhouses
And lean over the top to say a hurry-word through
      the glass
To your friends, the grapes, inside.

Lilacs,
False blue,
White,
Purple,
Color of lilac,
You have forgotten your Eastern origin,
The veiled women with eyes like panthers,
The swollen, aggressive turbans of jeweled Pashas.
Now you are a very decent flower,
A reticent flower,
A curiously clear-cut, candid flower,
Standing beside clean doorways,
Friendly to a house-cat and a pair of spectacles,
Making poetry out of a bit of moonlight
And a hundred or two sharp blossoms.

Maine knows you,
Has for years and years;
New Hampshire knows you,
And Massachusetts
And Vermont.

Amy Lowell

Cape Cod starts you along the beaches to Rhode
    Island;
Connecticut takes you from a river to the sea.
You are brighter than apples,
Sweeter than tulips,
You are the great flood of our souls
Bursting above the leaf-shapes of our hearts,
You are the smell of all Summers,
The love of wives and children,
The recollection of the gardens of little children,
You are State Houses and Charters
And the familiar treading of the foot to and fro on
  ·   a road it knows.
May is lilac here in New England,
May is a thrush singing " Sun up!" on a tip-top
    ash-tree,
May is white clouds behind pine-trees
Puffed out and marching upon a blue sky.
May is a green as no other,
May is much sun through small leaves,
May is soft earth,
And apple-blossoms,
And windows open to a South wind.
May is a full light wind of lilac
From Canada to Narragansett Bay.

Lilacs,
False blue,
White,
Purple,
6

Amy Lowell

Color of lilac,
Heart-leaves of lilac all over New England,
Roots of lilac under all the soil of New England,
Lilac in me because I am New England,
Because my roots are in it,
Because my leaves are of it,
Because my flowers are for it,
Because it is my country
And I speak to it of itself
And sing of it with my own voice
Since certainly it is mine.

Amy Lowell

TWENTY-FOUR HOKKU ON A MODERN THEME

I

AGAIN the larkspur,
Heavenly blue in my garden.
They, at least, unchanged.

II

How have I hurt you?
You look at me with pale eyes,
But these are my tears.

III

Morning and evening—
Yet for us once long ago
Was no division.

IV

I hear many words.
Set an hour when I may come
Or remain silent.

V

In the ghostly dawn
I write new words for your ears—
Even now you sleep.

Amy Lowell

VI

This then is morning.
Have you no comfort for me
Cold-colored flowers?

VII

My eyes are weary
Following you everywhere.
Short, oh short, the days!

VIII

When the flower falls
The leaf is no more cherished.
Every day I fear.

IX

Even when you smile
Sorrow is behind your eyes.
Pity me, therefore.

X

Laugh—it is nothing.
To others you may seem gay,
I watch with grieved eyes.

Amy Lowell

XI

Take it, this white rose.
Stems of roses do not bleed;
Your fingers are safe.

XII

As a river-wind
Hurling clouds at a bright moon,
So am I to you.

XIII

Watching the iris,
The faint and fragile petals—
How am I worthy?

XIV

Down a red river
I drift in a broken skiff.
Are you then so brave?

XV

Night lies beside me
Chaste and cold as a sharp sword.
It and I alone.

XVI

Last night it rained.
Now, in the desolate dawn,
Crying of blue jays.

Amy Lowell

XVII

Foolish so to grieve,
Autumn has its colored leaves—
But before they turn?

XVIII

Afterwards I think:
Poppies bloom when it thunders.
Is this not enough?

XIX

Love is a game—yes?
I think it is a drowning:
Black willows and stars.

XX

When the aster fades
The creeper flaunts in crimson.
Always another!

XXI

Turning from the page,
Blind with a night of labor,
I hear morning crows.

XXII

A cloud of lilies,
Or else you walk before me.
Who could see clearly?

Amy Lowell

XXIII

Sweet smell of wet flowers
Over an evening garden.
Your portrait, perhaps?

XXIV

Staying in my room,
I thought of the new Spring leaves.
That day was happy.

Amy Lowell

THE SWANS

THE swans float and float
Along the moat
Around the Bishop's garden,
And the white clouds push
Across a blue sky
With edges that seem to draw in and harden.

Two slim men of white bronze
Beat each with a hammer on the end of a rod
The hours of God.
Striking a bell,
They do it well.
And the echoes jump, and tinkle, and swell
In the Cathedral's carved stone polygons.

The swans float
About the moat,
And another swan sits still in the air
Above the old inn.
He gazes into the street
And swims the cold and the heat,
He has always been there,
At least so say the cobbles in the square.
They listen to the beat
Of the hammered bell,
And think of the feet
Which beat upon their tops;
But what they think they do not tell.

13

Amy Lowell

And the swans who float
Up and down the moat
Gobble the bread the Bishop feeds them.
The slim bronze men beat the hour again,
But only the gargoyles up in the hard blue air heed
     them.

When the Bishop says a prayer,
And the choir sing " Amen,"
The hammers break in on them there:
Clang! Clang! Beware! Beware!
The carved swan looks down at the passing men,
And the cobbles wink: " An hour has gone again."
But the people kneeling before the Bishop's chair
Forget the passing over the cobbles in the square.

An hour of day and an hour of night,
And the clouds float away in a red-splashed light.
The sun, quotha? or white, white
Smoke with fire all alight.

An old roof crashing on a Bishop's tomb,
Swarms of men with a thirst for room,
And the footsteps blur to a shower, shower, shower,
Of men passing—passing—every hour,
With arms of power, and legs of power,
And power in their strong, hard minds.
No need then
For the slim bronze men
Who beat God's hours: Prime, Tierce, None.
Who wants to hear?   No one.
14

We will melt them, and mold them,
And make them a stem
For a banner gorged with blood,
For a blue-mouthed torch.
So the men rush like clouds,
They strike their iron edges on the Bishop's chair
And fling down the lanterns by the tower stair.
They rip the Bishop out of his tomb
And break the mitre off of his head.
" See," say they, " the man is dead;
He cannot shiver or sing.
We'll toss for his ring."

The cobbles see this all along the street
Coming—coming—on countless feet.
And the clockmen mark the hours as they go.
But slow—slow—
The swans float
In the Bishop's moat.
And the inn swan
Sits on and on,
Staring before him with cold glass eyes.
Only the Bishop walks serene,
Pleased with his church, pleased with his house,
Pleased with the sound of the hammered bell,
Beating his doom.
Saying " Boom! Boom! Room! Room! "
He is old, and kind, and deaf, and blind,
And very, very pleased with his charming moat
And the swans which float.

15

Amy Lowell

PRIME

YOUR voice is like bells over roofs at dawn
When a bird flies
And the sky changes to a fresher color.

Speak, speak, Beloved.
Say little things
For my ears to catch
And run with them to my heart.

Amy Lowell

VESPERS

LAST night, at sunset,
The foxgloves were like tall altar candles.
Could I have lifted you to the roof of the green-
        house, my Dear,
I should have understood their burning.

Amy Lowell

IN EXCELSIS

You—you—
Your shadow is sunlight on a plate of silver;
Your footsteps, the seeding-place of lilies;
Your hands moving, a chime of bells across a wind-
    less air.

The movement of your hands is the long, golden
    running of light from a rising sun;
It is the hopping of birds upon a garden-path.

As the perfume of jonquils, you come forth in the
    morning.
Young horses are not more sudden than your
    thoughts,
Your words are bees about a pear-tree,
Your fancies are the gold-and-black striped wasps
    buzzing among red apples.
I drink your lips,
I eat the whiteness of your hands and feet.
My mouth is open,
As a new jar I am empty and open.
Like white water are you who fill the cup of my
    mouth,
Like a brook of water thronged with lilies.

You are frozen as the clouds,
You are far and sweet as the high clouds.
18

Amy Lowell

I dare reach to you,
I dare touch the rim of your brightness.
I leap beyond the winds,
I cry and shout,
For my throat is keen as a sword
Sharpened on a hone of ivory.
My throat sings the joy of my eyes,
The rushing gladness of my love.

How has the rainbow fallen upon my heart?
How have I snared the seas to lie in my fingers
And caught the sky to be a cover for my head?
How have you come to dwell with me,
Compassing me with the four circles of your mystic
        lightness,
So that I say "Glory! Glory!" and bow before you
As to a shrine?

Do I tease myself that morning is morning and a day
        after?
Do I think the air a condescension,
The earth a politeness,
Heaven a boon deserving thanks?
So you—air—earth—heaven—
I do not thank you,
I take you,
I live.
And those things which I say in consequence
Are rubies mortised in a gate of stone.

Amy Lowell

LA RONDE DU DIABLE

" HERE we go round the ivy-bush,"
And that's a tune we all dance to.
Little poet people snatching ivy,
Trying to prevent one another from snatching ivy.
If you get a leaf, there's another for me;
Look at the bush.
But I want your leaf, Brother, and you mine,
Therefore, of course, we push.

" Here we go round the laurel-tree."
Do we want laurels for ourselves most,
Or most that no one else shall have any?
We cannot stop to discuss the question.
We cannot stop to plait them into crowns
Or notice whether they become us.
We scarcely see the laurel-tree,
The crowd about us is all we see,
And there's no room in it for you and me.
Therefore, Sisters, it's my belief
We've none of us very much chance at a leaf.

" Here we go round the barberry-bush."
It's a bitter, blood-red fruit at best.
Which puckers the mouth and burns the heart.
To tell the truth, only one or two
Want the berries enough to strive
For more than he has, more than she.
An acid berry for you and me.
20

Amy Lowell

Abundance of berries for all who will eat,
But an aching meat.
That's poetry.
And who wants to swallow a mouthful of sorrow?
The world is old and our century
Must be well along, and we've no time to waste.
Make haste, Brothers and Sisters, push
With might and main round the ivy-bush,
Struggle and pull at the laurel-tree,
And leave the barberries be
For poor lost lunatics like me,
Who set them so high
They overtop the sun in the sky.
Does it matter at all that we don't know why?

21

ROBERT FROST

Robert Frost

FIRE AND ICE

SOME say the world will end in fire,
    Some say in ice.
From what I've tasted of desire
I hold with those who favor fire.
    But if it had to perish twice,
I think I know enough of hate
    To know that for destruction ice
Is also great,
    And would suffice.

Robert Frost

THE GRINDSTONE

HAVING a wheel and four legs of its own
Has never availed the cumbersome grindstone
To get it anywhere that I can see.
These hands have helped it go and even race;
Not all the motion, though, they ever lent,
Not all the miles it may have thought it went,
Have got it one step from the starting place.
It stands beside the same old apple tree.
The shadow of the apple tree is thin
Upon it now; its feet are fast in snow.
All other farm machinery's gone in,
And some of it on no more legs and wheel
Than the grindstone can boast to stand or go.
(I'm thinking chiefly of the wheelbarrow.)
For months it hasn't known the taste of steel,
Washed down with rusty water in a tin.
But standing outdoors, hungry, in the cold,
Except in towns, at night, is not a sin.
And, anyway, its standing in the yard
Under a ruinous live apple tree
Has nothing any more to do with me,
Except that I remember how of old,
One summer day, all day I drove it hard,
And some one mounted on it rode it hard,
And he and I between us ground a blade.

I gave it the preliminary spin,
And poured on water (tears it might have been);

Robert Frost

And when it almost gayly jumped and flowed,
A Father-Time-like man got on and rode,
Armed with a scythe and spectacles that glowed.
He turned on will-power to increase the load
And slow me down—and I abruptly slowed,
Like coming to a sudden railroad station.
I changed from hand to hand in desperation.

I wondered what machine of ages gone
This represented an improvement on.
For all I knew it may have sharpened spears
And arrowheads itself. Much use for years
Had gradually worn it an oblate
Spheroid that kicked and struggled in its gait,
Appearing to return me hate for hate.
(But I forgive it now as easily
As any other boyhood enemy
Whose pride has failed to get him anywhere.)
I wondered who it was the man thought ground—
The one who held the wheel back or the one
Who gave his life to keep it going round?
I wondered if he really thought it fair
For him to have the say when we were done.
Such were the bitter thoughts to which I turned.

Not for myself was I so much concerned.
Oh, no!—although, of course, I could have found
A better way to pass the afternoon
Than grinding discord out of a grindstone,
And beating insects at their gritty tune.

27

Nor was I for the man so much concerned.
Once when the grindstone almost jumped its bearing
It looked as if he might be badly thrown
And wounded on his blade. So far from caring,
I laughed inside, and only cranked the faster,
(It ran as if it wasn't greased but glued);
I welcomed any moderate disaster
That might be calculated to postpone
What evidently nothing could conclude.

The thing that made me more and more afraid
Was that we'd ground it sharp and hadn't known,
And now were only wasting precious blade.
And when he raised it dripping once and tried
The creepy edge of it with wary touch,
And viewed it over his glasses funny-eyed,
Only disinterestedly to decide
It needed a turn more, I could have cried
Wasn't there danger of a turn too much?
Mightn't we make it worse instead of better?
I was for leaving something to the whetter.
What if it wasn't all it should be? I'd
Be satisfied if he'd be satisfied.

Robert Frost

THE WITCH OF COÖS

Circa 1922

I STAID the night for shelter at a farm
Behind the mountain, with a mother and son,
Two old-believers. They did all the talking.

The Mother

Folks think a witch who has familiar spirits
She *could* call up to pass a winter evening,
But *won't,* should be burned at the stake or
    something.
Summoning spirits isn't " Button, button,
Who's got the button? " I'd have you under-
    stand.

The Son

Mother can make a common table rear
And kick with two legs like an army mule.

The Mother

And when I've done it, what good have I done?
Rather than tip a table for you, let me
Tell you what Ralle the Sioux Control once
    told me.
He said the dead had souls, but when I asked
    him
How that could be—I thought the dead were
    souls,

29

He broke my trance. Don't that make you
    suspicious
That there's something the dead are keeping
    back?
Yes, there's something the dead are keeping
    back.

The Son

You wouldn't want to tell him what we have
Up attic, mother?

The Mother

                        Bones—a skeleton.

The Son

But the headboard of mother's bed is pushed
Against the attic door: the door is nailed.
It's harmless. Mother hears it in the night
Halting perplexed behind the barrier
Of door and headboard. Where it wants to get
Is back into the cellar where it came from.

The Mother

We'll never let them, will we, son? We'll never!

The Son

It left the cellar forty years ago
And carried itself like a pile of dishes
Up one flight from the cellar to the kitchen,
Another from the kitchen to the bedroom,
Another from the bedroom to the attic,

Right past both father and mother, and neither
  stopped it.
Father had gone upstairs; mother was down-
  stairs.
I was a baby: I don't know where I was.

The Mother

The only fault my husband found with me—
I went to sleep before I went to bed,
Especially in winter when the bed
Might just as well be ice and the clothes snow.
The night the bones came up the cellar-stairs
Toffile had gone to bed alone and left me,
But left an open door to cool the room off
So as to sort of turn me out of it.
I was just coming to myself enough
To wonder where the cold was coming from,
When I heard Toffile upstairs in the bedroom
And thought I heard him downstairs in the
  cellar.
The board we had laid down to walk dry-shod on
When there was water in the cellar in spring
Struck the hard cellar bottom. And then some
  one
Began the stairs, two footsteps for each step,
The way a man with one leg and a crutch,
Or little child, comes up. It wasn't Toffile:
It wasn't any one who could be there.
The bulkhead double-doors were double-locked
And swollen tight and buried under snow.

31

Robert Frost

The cellar windows were banked up with saw-
     dust
And swollen tight and buried under snow.
It was the bones. I knew them—and good
     reason.
My first impulse was to get to the knob
And hold the door. But the bones didn't try
The door; they halted helpless on the landing,
Waiting for things to happen in their favor.
The faintest restless rustling ran all through
     them.
I never could have done the thing I did
If the wish hadn't been too strong in me
To see how they were mounted for this walk.
I had a vision of them put together
Not like a man, but like a chandelier.
So suddenly I flung the door wide on him.
A moment he stood balancing with emotion,
And all but lost himself. (A tongue of fire
Flashed out and licked along his upper teeth.
Smoke rolled inside the sockets of his eyes.)
Then he came at me with one hand outstretched,
The way he did in life once; but this time
I struck the hand off brittle on the floor,
And fell back from him on the floor myself.
The finger-pieces slid in all directions.
(Where did I see one of those pieces lately?
Hand me my button-box—it must be there.)

I sat up on the floor and shouted, " Toffile,
It's coming up to you."   It had its choice
Of the door to the cellar or the hall.
It took the hall door for the novelty,
And set off briskly for so slow a thing,
Still going every which way in the joints, though,
So that it looked like lightning or a scribble,
From the slap I had just now given its hand.
I listened till it almost climbed the stairs
From the hall to the only finished bedroom,
Before I got up to do anything;
Then ran and shouted, " Shut the bedroom
          door,
Toffile, for my sake! "   " Company," he said,
" Don't make me get up; I'm too warm in bed."
So lying forward weakly on the handrail
I pushed myself upstairs, and in the light
(The kitchen had been dark) I had to own
I could see nothing. " Toffile, I don't see it.
It's with us in the room, though.   It's the
          bones."
" What bones? "   " The cellar bones—out of
          the grave."

That made him throw his bare legs out of bed
And sit up by me and take hold of me.
I wanted to put out the light and see

If I could see it, or else mow the room,
With our arms at the level of our knees,
And bring the chalk-pile down. " I'll tell you
     what—
It's looking for another door to try.
The uncommonly deep snow has made him
     think
Of his old song, *The Wild Colonial Boy,*
He always used to sing along the tote-road.
He's after an open door to get out-doors.
Let's trap him with an open door up attic."
Toffile agreed to that, and sure enough,
Almost the moment he was given an opening,
The steps began to climb the attic stairs.
I heard them. Toffile didn't seem to hear them.
" Quick!" I slammed to the door and held the
     knob.
" Toffile, get nails." I made him nail the door
     shut,
And push the headboard of the bed against it.

Then we asked was there anything
Up attic that we'd ever want again.
The attic was less to us than the cellar.
If the bones liked the attic, let them like it,
Let them *stay* in the attic. When they some-
     times
Come down the stairs at night and stand per-
     plexed
Behind the door and headboard of the bed,

Robert Frost

Brushing their chalky skull with chalky fingers,
With sounds like the dry rattling of a shutter,
That's what I sit up in the dark to say—
To no one any more since Toffile died.
Let them stay in the attic since they went there.
I promised Toffile to be cruel to them
For helping them be cruel once to him.

The Son
We think they had a grave down in the cellar.

The Mother
We know they had a grave down in the cellar.

The Son
We never could find out whose bones they were.

The Mother
Yes, we could too, son. Tell the truth for once.
They were a man's his father killed for me.
I mean a man he killed instead of me.
The least I could do was to help dig their grave.
We were about it one night in the cellar.
Son knows the story: but 'twas not for him
To tell the truth, suppose the time had come.
Son looks surprised to see me end a lie
We'd kept up all these years between ourselves
So as to have it ready for outsiders.
But to-night I don't care enough to lie—
I don't remember why I ever cared.

Robert Frost

Toffile, if he were here, I don't believe
Could tell you why he ever cared himself. . . .

She hadn't found the finger-bone she wanted
Among the buttons poured out in her lap.

I verified the name next morning: Toffile;
The rural letter-box said Toffile Lajway.

Robert Frost

A BROOK IN THE CITY

THE farm house lingers, though averse to square
With the new city street it has to wear
A number in.   But what about the brook
That held the house as in an elbow-crook?
I ask as one who knew the brook, its strength
And impulse, having dipped a finger-length
And made it leap my knuckle, having tossed
A flower to try its currents where they crossed.
The meadow grass could be cemented down
From growing under pavements of a town;
The apple trees be sent to hearth-stone flame.
Is water wood to serve a brook the same?
How else dispose of an immortal force
No longer needed?   Staunch it at its source
With cinder loads dumped down?   The brook was
        thrown
Deep in a sewer dungeon under stone
In fetid darkness still to live and run—
And all for nothing it had ever done
Except forget to go in fear perhaps.
No one would know except for ancient maps
That such a brook ran water.   But I wonder
If, from its being kept forever under,
These thoughts may not have risen that so keep
This new-built city from both work and sleep.

Robert Frost

DESIGN

I FOUND a dimpled spider, fat and white,
On a white heal-all, holding up a moth
Like a white piece of rigid satin cloth—
Assorted characters of death and blight
Mixed ready to begin the morning right,
Like the ingredients of a witches' broth—
A snow-drop spider, a flower like froth,
And dead wings carried like a paper kite.

What had that flower to do with being white,
The wayside blue and innocent heal-all?
What brought the kindred spider to that height,
Then steered the white moth thither in the night?
What but design of darkness to appal?—
If design govern in a thing so small.

CARL SANDBURG

Carl Sandburg

AND SO TO-DAY

AND so to-day—they lay him away—
the boy nobody knows the name of—
the buck private—the unknown soldier—
the doughboy who dug under and died
when they told him to—that's him.

Down Pennsylvania Avenue to-day the riders go,
men and boys riding horses, roses in their teeth,
stems of roses, rose leaf stalks, rose dark leaves—
the line of the green ends in a red rose flash.

Skeleton men and boys riding skeleton horses,
the rib bones shine, the rib bones curve,
shine with savage, elegant curves—
a jawbone runs with a long white slant,
a skull dome runs with a long white arch,
bone triangles click and rattle,
elbows, ankles, white line slants—
shining in the sun, past the White House,
past the Treasury Building, Army and Navy Build-
        ings,
on to the mystic white Capitol Dome—
so they go down Pennsylvania Avenue to-day,
skeleton men and boys riding skeleton horses,
stems of roses in their teeth,
rose dark leaves at their white jaw slants—
and a horse laugh question nickers and whinnies,

moans with a whistle out of horse head teeth:
why? who? where?

  (" The big fish—eat the little fish—
    the little fish—eat the shrimps—
    and the shrimps—eat mud,"—
    said a cadaverous man—with a black umbrella—
    spotted with white polka dots—with a missing
    ear—with a missing foot and arms—
    with a missing sheath of muscles
    singing to the silver sashes of the sun.)

And so to-day—they lay him away—
the boy nobody knows the name of—
the buck private—the unknown soldier—
the doughboy who dug under and died
when they told him to—that's him.

If he picked himself and said, " I am ready to die,"
if he gave his name and said, "My country, take me,"
then the baskets of roses to-day are for the Boy,
the flowers, the songs, the steamboat whistles,
the proclamations of the honorable orators,
they are all for the Boy—that's him.

If the government of the Republic picked him saying,
" You are wanted, your country takes you "—
if the Republic put a stethoscope to his heart
and looked at his teeth and tested his eyes and said,
" You are a citizen of the Republic and a sound

42

animal in all parts and functions—the Republic
    takes you "—
then to-day the baskets of flowers are all for the
    Republic,
the roses, the songs, the steamboat whistles,
the proclamations of the honorable orators—
they are all for the Republic.

And so to-day—they lay him away—
and an understanding goes—his long sleep shall be
under arms and arches near the Capitol Dome—
there is an authorization—he shall have tomb com-
    panions—
the martyred presidents of the Republic—
the buck private—the unknown soldier—that's him.

The man who was war commander of the armies of
    the Republic
rides down Pennsylvania Avenue—
The man who is peace commander of the armies of
    the Republic
rides down Pennsylvania Avenue—
for the sake of the Boy, for the sake of the Republic.

  (And the hoofs of the skeleton horses
    all drum soft on the asphalt footing—
    so soft is the drumming, so soft the roll call
    of the grinning sergeants calling the roll call—
    so soft is it all—a camera man murmurs, " Moon-
        shine.")

Carl Sandburg

Look—who salutes the coffin—
lays a wreath of remembrance
on the box where a buck private
sleeps a clean dry sleep at last—
look—it is the highest ranking general
of the officers of the armies of the Republic.

> (Among pigeon corners of the Congressional Li-
> brary—they file documents quietly, casually, all
> in a day's work—this human document, the
> buck private nobody knows the name of—they
> file away in granite and steel—with music and
> roses, salutes, proclamations of the honorable
> orators.)

Across the country, between two ocean shore lines,
where cities cling to rail and water routes,
there people and horses stop in their foot tracks,
cars and wagons stop in their wheel tracks—
faces at street crossings shine with a silence
of eggs laid in a row on a pantry shelf—
among the ways and paths of the flow of the Republic
faces come to a standstill, sixty clockticks count—
in the name of the Boy, in the name of the Republic.

> (A million faces a thousand miles from Pennsyl-
> vania Avenue
> stay frozen with a look, a clocktick, a moment—
> skeleton riders on skeleton horses—the nicker-
> ing high horse laugh,

the whinny and the howl up Pennsylvania Ave-
   nue: who? why? where?)

(So people far from the asphalt footing of
Pennsylvania Avenue look, wonder, mumble—
the riding white-jaw phantoms ride hi-eeee,
hi-eeee, hi-yi, hi-yi, hi-eeee—the proclamations
of the honorable orators mix with the top-
sergeants whistling the roll call.)

If when the clockticks counted sixty,
when the heartbeats of the Republic
came to a stop for a minute,
if the Boy had happened to sit up,
happening to sit up as Lazarus sat up, in the story,
then the first shivering language to drip off his mouth
might have come as, " Thank God," or " Am I
      dreaming? "
or " What the hell " or " When do we eat? "
or " Kill 'em, kill 'em, the . . ."
or " Was that . . . a rat . . . ran over my face? "
or " For Christ's sake, gimme water, gimme water,"
or " Blub blub, bloo bloo. . . . . . ."
or any bubbles of shell shock gibberish
from the gashes of No Man's Land.

Maybe some buddy knows,
some sister, mother, sweetheart,
maybe some girl who sat with him once
when a two-horn silver moon

slid on the peak of a house-roof gable,
and promises lived in the air of the night,
when the air was filled with promises,
when any little slip-shoe lovey
could pick a promise out of the air.

      " Feed it to 'em,
      they lap it up,
      bull . . . bull . . . bull,"
Said a movie news reel camera man,
Said a Washington newspaper correspondent,
Said a baggage handler lugging a trunk,
Said a two-a-day vaudeville juggler,
Said a hanky-pank selling jumping-jacks.
" Hokum—they lap it up," said the bunch.

And a tall scar-face ball player,
Played out as a ball player,
Made a speech of his own for the hero boy,
Sent an earful of his own to the dead buck private:
      " It's all safe now, buddy,
      Safe when you say yes,
      Safe for the yes-men."

He was a tall scar-face battler
With his face in a newspaper
Reading want ads, reading jokes,
Reading love, murder, politics,
Jumping from jokes back to the want ads,
Reading the want ads first and last,
46

Carl Sandburg

The letters of the word JOB, " J-O-B,"
Burnt like a shot of bootleg booze
In the bones of his head—
In the wish of his scar-face eyes.

The honorable orators,
Always the honorable orators,
Buttoning the buttons on their prinz alberts,
Pronouncing the syllables " sac-ri-fice,"
Juggling those bitter salt-soaked syllables—
Do they ever gag with hot ashes in their mouths?
Do their tongues ever shrivel with a pain of fire
Across those simple syllables " sac-ri-fice "?

(There was one orator people far off saw.
He had on a gunnysack shirt over his bones,
And he lifted an elbow socket over his head,
And he lifted a skinny signal finger.
And he had nothing to say, nothing easy—
He mentioned ten million men, mentioned them as
        having gone west, mentioned them as shoving
        up the daisies.
We could write it all on a postage stamp, what he
        said.
He said it and quit and faded away,
A gunnysack shirt on his bones.)

>   Stars of the night sky,
>   did you see that phantom fadeout,
>   did you see those phantom riders,

Carl Sandburg

skeleton riders on skeleton horses,
stems of roses in their teeth,
rose leaves red on white-jaw slants,
grinning along on Pennsylvania Avenue,
the top-sergeants calling roll calls—
did their horses nicker a horse laugh?
did the ghosts of the boney battalions
move out and on, up the Potomac, over on the
         Ohio
and out to the Mississippi, the Missouri, the
         Red River,
and down to the Rio Grande, and on to the
         Yazoo,
over to the Chattahoochee and up to the Rappa-
         hannock?
did you see 'em, stars of the night sky?

And so to-day—they lay him away—
the boy nobody knows the name of—
they lay him away in granite and steel—
with music and roses—under a flag—
under a sky of promises.

Carl Sandburg

CALIFORNIA CITY LANDSCAPE

On a mountain-side the real estate agents
Put up signs marking the city lots to be sold there.
A man whose father and mother were Irish
Ran a goat farm half-way down the mountain;
He drove a covered wagon years ago,
Understood how to handle a rifle,
Shot grouse, buffalo, Indians, in a single year,
And now was raising goats around a shanty.
Down at the foot of the mountain
Two Japanese families had flower farms.
A man and woman were in rows of sweet peas
Picking the pink and white flowers
To put in baskets and take to the Los Angeles
    market.
They were clean as what they handled
There in the morning sun, the big people and the
    baby-faces.
Across the road, high on another mountain,
Stood a house saying, " I am it," a commanding
    house.
There was the home of a motion picture director
Famous for lavish whore-house interiors,
Clothes ransacked from the latest designs for women
In the combats of " male against female."
The mountain, the scenery, the layout of the land-
    scape,
And the peace of the morning sun as it happened,

49

Carl Sandburg

The miles of houses pocketed in the valley beyond—
It was all worth looking at, worth wondering about,
How long it might last, how young it might be.

Carl Sandburg

UPSTREAM

THE strong men keep coming on.
They go down shot, hanged, sick, broken.
They live on, fighting, singing,
   lucky as plungers.

The strong men . . . they keep coming on.
The strong mothers pulling them
   from a dark sea, a great prairie,
   a long mountain.

Call hallelujah, call amen,
   call deep thanks.
The strong men keep coming on.

Carl Sandburg

WINDFLOWER LEAF

THIS flower is repeated
out of old winds, out of
old times.

The wind repeats these, it
must have these, over and
over again.

Oh, windflowers so fresh,
Oh, beautiful leaves, here
now again.

   The domes over
   fall to pieces.
   The stones under
   fall to pieces.
   Rain and ice
   wreck the works.
The wind keeps, the windflowers
   keep, the leaves last,
The wind young and strong lets
   these last longer than stones.

VACHEL LINDSAY

Vachel Lindsay

IN PRAISE OF JOHNNY APPLESEED[1]

(Born 1775. Died 1847)

I. OVER THE APPALACHIAN BARRICADE

IN the days of President Washington,
The glory of the nations,
Dust and ashes,
Snow and sleet,
And hay and oats and wheat,
Blew west,
Crossed the Appalachians,
Found the glades of rotting leaves, the soft deer-
      pastures,
The farms of the far-off future
In the forest.
Colts jumped the fence,
Snorting, ramping, snapping, sniffing,
With gastronomic calculations,
Crossed the Appalachians,
The east walls of our citadel,
And turned to gold-horned unicorns,
Feasting in the dim, volunteer farms of the forest.
Stripedest, kickingest kittens escaped,
Caterwauling " Yankee Doodle Dandy,"

To be read like old leaves on the elm tree of Time. Sifting soft winds with sentence and rhyme.

[1] The best account of John Chapman's career, under the name "Johnny Appleseed," is to be found in *Harper's Monthly Magazine*, November, 1871.

55

Vachel Lindsay

Renounced their poor relations,
Crossed the Appalachians,
And turned to tiny tigers
In the humorous forest.
Chickens escaped
From farmyard congregations,
Crossed the Appalachians,
And turned to amber trumpets
On the ramparts of our Hoosiers' nest and citadel,
Millennial heralds
Of the foggy mazy forest.
Pigs broke loose, scrambled west,
Scorned their loathsome stations,
Crossed the Appalachians,
Turned to roaming, foaming wild boars
Of the forest.
The smallest, blindest puppies toddled west
While their eyes were coming open,
And, with misty observations,
Crossed the Appalachians,
Barked, barked, barked
At the glow-worms and the marsh lights and the
        lightning-bugs,
And turned to ravening wolves
Of the forest.
Crazy parrots and canaries flew west,
Drunk on May-time revelations,
Crossed the Appalachians,
And turned to delirious, flower-dressed fairies
Of the lazy forest.

Haughtiest swans and peacocks swept west,
And, despite soft derivations,
Crossed the Appalachians,
And turned to blazing warrior souls
Of the forest,
Singing the ways
Of the Ancient of Days.
And the " Old Continentals
In their ragged regimentals,"
With bard's imaginations,
Crossed the Appalachians.
And
A boy
Blew west
And with prayers and incantations,
And with " Yankee Doodle Dandy,"
Crossed the Appalachians,
And was " young John Chapman,"
Then
" Johnny Appleseed, Johnny Appleseed,"
Chief of the fastnesses, dappled and vast,
In a pack on his back,
In a deer-hide sack,
The beautiful orchards of the past,
The ghosts of all the forests and the groves—
In that pack on his back,
In that talisman sack,
To-morrow's peaches, pears and cherries,
To-morrow's grapes and red raspberries,
Seeds and tree souls, precious things,

Vachel Lindsay

Feathered with microscopic wings,
All the outdoors the child heart knows,
And the apple, green, red, and white,
Sun of his day and his night—
The apple allied to the thorn,
Child of the rose.
Porches untrod of forest houses
All before him, all day long,
" Yankee Doodle " his marching song;
And the evening breeze
Joined his psalms of praise
As he sang the ways
Of the Ancient of Days.

Leaving behind august Virginia,
Proud Massachusetts, and proud Maine,
Planting the trees that would march and train
On, in his name to the great Pacific,
Like Birnam wood to Dunsinane,
Johnny Appleseed swept on,
Every shackle gone,
Loving every sloshy brake,
Loving every skunk and snake,
Loving every leathery weed,
Johnny Appleseed, Johnny Appleseed,
Master and ruler of the unicorn-ramping forest,
The tiger-mewing forest,
The rooster-trumpeting, boar-foaming, wolf-raven-
    ing forest,
The spirit-haunted, fairy-enchanted forest,
58

Vachel Lindsay

tupendous and endless,
earching its perilous ways
n the name of the Ancient of Days.

II. THE INDIANS WORSHIP HIM, BUT HE
HURRIES ON

Painted kings in the midst of the clearing
Heard him asking his friends the eagles
To guard each planted seed and seedling.
Then he was a god, to the red man's dreaming;
Then the chiefs brought treasures grotesque and
        fair,—
Magical trinkets and pipes and guns,
Beads and furs from their medicine-lair,—
Stuck holy feathers in his hair,
Hailed him with austere delight.
The orchard god was their guest through the night.

While the late snow blew from bleak Lake Erie,
Scourging rock and river and reed,
All night long they made great medicine
For Jonathan Chapman,
Johnny Appleseed,
Johnny Appleseed;
And as though his heart were a wind-blown wheat-
        sheaf,

59

Vachel Lindsay

As though his heart were a new-built nest,
As though their heaven house were his breast,
In swept the snow-birds singing glory.
And I hear his bird heart beat its story,
Hear yet how the ghost of the forest shivers,
Hear yet the cry of the gray, old orchards,
Dim and decaying by the rivers,
And the timid wings of the bird-ghosts beating,
And the ghosts of the tom-toms beating, beating.

But he left their wigwams and their love. *While   you*
By the hour of dawn he was proud and *read,   hear*
    stark,   *the   hoof-*
                                        beats of deer
Kissed the Indian babes with a sigh, *in the snow.*
Went forth to live on roots and bark, *And see, by*
                                       their . track,
Sleep in the trees, while the years howled *bleeding*
    by—   *footprints*
                                       we know.

Calling the catamounts by name,
And buffalo bulls no hand could tame,
Slaying never a living creature,
Joining the birds in every game,
With the gorgeous turkey gobblers mocking,
With the lean-necked eagles boxing and shouting;
Sticking their feathers in his hair,—
Turkey feathers,
Eagle feathers,—
Trading hearts with all beasts and weathers
He swept on, winged and wonder-crested,
Bare-armed, barefooted, and bare-breasted.

Vachel Lindsay

The maples, shedding their spinning
    seeds,
Called to his appleseeds in the ground,
Vast chestnut-trees, with their butterfly
    nations,
Called to his seeds without a sound.
And the chipmunk turned a " summer-
    set,"
And the foxes danced the Virginia reel;
Hawthorne and crab-thorn bent, rain-wet,
And dropped their flowers in his night-black hair;
And the soft fawns stopped for his perorations;
And his black eyes shone through the forest-gleam,
And he plunged young hands into new-turned earth,
And prayed dear orchard boughs into birth;
And he ran with the rabbit and slept with the stream.
And he ran with the rabbit and slept with the stream.
And so for us he made great medicine,
And so for us he made great medicine,
In the days of President Washington.

While you read, see conventions of deer go by. The bucks toss their horns, the fuzzy fawns fly.

III. JOHNNY APPLESEED'S OLD AGE

Long, long after,
When settlers put up beam and rafter,
They asked of the birds: " Who gave this fruit?
Who watched this fence till the seeds took root?
Who gave these boughs? " They asked the sky,
And there was no reply.
But the robin might have said,

To be read like faint hoof-beats

61

Vachel Lindsay

" To the farthest West he has followed *of fawns*
       the sun, *long gone*
His life and his empire just begun." *From re-*
spectable
pasture, and
park and
lawn,
Self-scourged, like a monk, with a *And heart-*
beats of
       throne for wages, *fawns that*
Stripped like the iron-souled Hindu sages, *are coming*
again
Draped like a statue, in strings like a *When the*
forest, once
      scarecrow, *more, is the*
His helmet-hat an old tin pan, *master of*
But worn in the love of the heart of man, *men.*
More sane than the helm of Tamerlane,
Hairy Ainu, wild man of Borneo, Robinson Crusoe
      —Johnny Appleseed;
And the robin might have said,
" Sowing, he goes to the far, new West,
With the apple, the sun of his burning breast—
The apple allied to the thorn,
Child of the rose."

Washington buried in Virginia,
Jackson buried in Tennessee,
Young Lincoln, brooding in Illinois,
And Johnny Appleseed, priestly and free,
Knotted and gnarled, past seventy years,
Still planted on in the woods alone.
Ohio and young Indiana—
These were his wide altar-stone,
Where still he burnt out flesh and bone.
62

Vachel Lindsay

Twenty days ahead of the Indian, twenty years
    ahead of the white man,
At last the Indian overtook him, at last the Indian
    hurried past him;
At last the white man overtook him, at last the white
    man hurried past him;
At last his own trees overtook him, at last his own
    trees hurried past him.
Many cats were tame again,
Many ponies tame again,
Many pigs were tame again,
Many canaries tame again;
And the real frontier was his sun-burnt breast.

From the fiery core of that apple, the earth,
Sprang apple-amaranths divine.
Love's orchards climbed to the heavens of the West,
And snowed the earthly sod with flowers.
Farm hands from the terraces of the blest
Danced on the mists with their ladies fine;
And Johnny Appleseed laughed with his dreams,
And swam once more the ice-cold streams.
And the doves of the spirit swept through the hours,
With doom-calls, love-calls, death-calls, dream-calls;
And Johnny Appleseed, all that year,
Lifted his hands to the farm-filled sky,
To the apple-harvesters busy on high;
And so once more his youth began,
And so for us he made great medicine—
Johnny Appleseed, medicine-man.

63

Then
The sun was his turned-up broken barrel,
Out of which his juicy apples rolled,
Down the repeated terraces,
Thumping across the gold,
An angel in each apple that touched the forest mold,
A ballot-box in each apple,
A state capital in each apple,
Great high schools, great colleges,
All America in each apple,
Each red, rich, round, and bouncing moon
That touched the forest mold.
Like scrolls and rolled-up flags of silk,
He saw the fruits unfold,
And all our expectations in one wild-flower-written
      dream,
Confusion and death sweetness, and a thicket of
      crab-thorns,
Heart of a hundred midnights, heart of the merciful
      morns.
Heaven's boughs bent down with their alchemy,
Perfumed airs, and thoughts of wonder.
And the dew on the grass and his own cold tears
Were one in brooding mystery,
Though death's loud thunder came upon him,
Though death's loud thunder struck him down—
The boughs and the proud thoughts swept through
      the thunder,
Till he saw our wide nation, each State a flower,
Each petal a park for holy feet,

Vachel Lindsay

With wild fawns merry on every street,
With wild fawns merry on every street,
The vista of ten thousand years, flower-lighted and
    complete.

Hear the lazy weeds murmuring, bays and rivers
    whispering,
From Michigan to Texas, California to Maine;
Listen to the eagles, screaming, calling,
" Johnny Appleseed, Johnny Appleseed,"
There by the doors of old Fort Wayne.

In the four-poster bed Johnny Appleseed built,
Autumn rains were the curtains, autumn leaves were
    the quilt.
He laid him down sweetly, and slept through the
    night,
Like a bump on a log, like a stone washed white,
There by the doors of old Fort Wayne.

Vachel Lindsay

I KNOW ALL THIS WHEN GIPSY
FIDDLES CRY

Oh, gipsies, proud and stiff-necked and perverse,
Saying: " We tell the fortunes of the nations,
And revel in the deep palm of the world.
The head-line is the road we choose for trade.
The love-line is the lane wherein we camp.
The life-line is the road we wander on.
Mount Venus, Jupiter, and all the rest
Are finger-tips of ranges clasping round
And holding up the Romany's wide sky."

Oh, gipsies, proud and stiff-necked and perverse,
Saying: " We will swap horses till the doom,
And mend the pots and kettles of mankind,
And lend our sons to big-time vaudeville,
Or to the race-track, or the learned world.
But India's Brahma waits within their breasts.
They will return to us with gipsy grins,
And chatter Romany, and shake their curls
And hug the dirtiest babies in the camp.
They will return to the moving pillar of smoke,
The whitest toothed, the merriest laughers known,
The blackest haired of all the tribes of men.
What trap can hold such cats? The Romany
Has crossed such delicate palms with lead or gold,
Wheedling in sun and rain, through perilous years,
All coins now look alike. The palm is all.
66

Vachel Lindsay

Our greasy pack of cards is still the book
Most read of men. The heart's librarians,
We tell all lovers what they want to know.
So, out of the famed Chicago Library,
Out of the great Chicago orchestras,
Out of the skyscraper, the Fine Arts Building,
Our sons will come with fiddles and with loot,
Dressed, as of old, like turkey-cocks and zebras,
Like tiger-lilies and chameleons,
Go west with us to California,
Telling the fortunes of the bleeding world,
And kiss the sunset, ere their day is done."

Oh, gipsies, proud and stiff-necked and perverse,
Picking the brains and pockets of mankind,
You will go westward for one-half hour yet.
You will turn eastward in a little while.
You will go back, as men turn to Kentucky,
Land of their fathers, dark and bloody ground.
When all the Jews go home to Syria,
When Chinese cooks go back to Canton, China,
When Japanese photographers return
With their black cameras to Tokio,
And Irish patriots to Donegal,
And Scotch accountants back to Edinburgh,
You will go back to India, whence you came.
When you have reached the borders of your quest,
Homesick at last, by many a devious way,
Winding the wonderlands circuitous,
By foot and horse will trace the long way back!

Vachel Lindsay

Fiddling for ocean liners, while the dance
Sweeps through the decks, your brown tribes all
　　will go!
Those east-bound ships will hear your long farewell
On fiddle, piccolo, and flute and timbrel.
I know all this, when gipsy fiddles cry.

That hour of their homesickness, I myself
Will turn, will say farewell to Illinois,
To old Kentucky and Virginia,
And go with them to India, whence they came.
For they have heard a singing from the Ganges,
And cries of orioles,—from the temple caves,—
And Bengal's oldest, humblest villages.
They smell the supper smokes of Amritsar.
Green monkeys cry in Sanskrit to their souls
From lofty bamboo trees of hot Madras.
They think of towns to ease their feverish eyes,
And make them stand and meditate forever,
Domes of astonishment, to heal the mind.
I know all this, when gipsy fiddles cry.

What music will be blended with the wind
When gipsy fiddlers, nearing that old land,
Bring tunes from all the world to Brahma's house?
Passing the Indus, winding poisonous forests,
Blowing soft flutes at scandalous temple girls,
Filling the highways with their magpie loot,
What brass from my Chicago will they heap,
What gems from Walla Walla, Omaha,

Vachel Lindsay

Will they pile near the Bodhi Tree, and laugh?
They will dance near such temples as best suit them,
Though they will not quite enter, or adore,
Looking on roofs, as poets look on lilies,
Looking at towers, as boys at forest vines,
That leap to tree-tops through the dizzy air.
I know all this, when gipsy fiddles cry.

And with the gipsies there will be a king
And a thousand desperadoes just his style,
With all their rags dyed in the blood of roses,
Splashed with the blood of angels, and of demons.
And he will boss them with an awful voice.
And with a red whip he will beat his wife.
He will be wicked on that sacred shore,
And rattle cruel spurs against the rocks,
And shake Calcutta's walls with circus bugles.
He will kill Brahmins there, in Kali's name,
And please the thugs, and blood-drunk of the earth.
I know all this, when gipsy fiddles cry.

Oh, sweating thieves, and hard-boiled scalawags,
That still will boast your pride until the doom,
Smashing every caste rule of the world,
Reaching at last your Hindu goal to smash
The caste rules of old India, and shout:
" Down with the Brahmins, let the Romany reign."

When gipsy girls look deep within my hand
They always speak so tenderly and say
That I am one of those star-crossed to wed

Vachel Lindsay

A princess in a forest fairy-tale.
So there will be a tender gipsy princess,
My Juliet, shining through this clan.
And I would sing you of her beauty now.
And I will fight with knives the gipsy man
Who tries to steal her wild young heart away.
And I will kiss her in the waterfalls,
And at the rainbow's end, and in the incense
That curls about the feet of sleeping gods,
And sing with her in canebrakes and in rice fields,
In Romany, eternal Romany.
We will sow secret herbs, and plant old roses,
And fumble through dark, snaky palaces,
Stable our ponies in the Taj Mahal,
And sleep out-doors ourselves.
In her strange fairy mill-wheel eyes will wait
All windings and unwindings of the highways,
From India, across America,—
All windings and unwindings of my fancy,
All windings and unwindings of all souls,
All windings and unwindings of the heavens.
I know all this, when gipsy fiddles cry.

We gipsies, proud and stiff-necked and perverse,
Standing upon the white Himalayas,
Will think of far divine Yosemite.
We will heal Hindu hermits there with oil
Brought from California's tall sequoias.
And we will be like gods that heap the thunders,
70

Vachel Lindsay

And start young redwood trees on Time's own moun-
    tains.
We will swap horses with the rising moon,
And mend that funny skillet called Orion,
Color the stars like San Francisco's street-lights,
And paint our sign and signature on high
In planets like a bed of crimson pansies;
While a million fiddles shake all listening hearts,
Crying good fortune to the Universe,
Whispering adventure to the Ganges waves,
And to the spirits, and all winds and gods.
Till mighty Brahma puts his golden palm
Within the gipsy king's great striped tent,
And asks his fortune told by that great love-line
That winds across his palm in splendid flame.

Only the hearthstone of old India
Will end the endless march of gipsy feet.
I will go back to India with them
When they go back to India whence they came.
I know all this, when gipsy fiddles cry.

JAMES OPPENHEIM

James Oppenheim

HEBREWS

I come of a mighty race. . . . I come of a very
    mighty race. . . .
Adam was a mighty man, and Noah a captain of the
    moving waters,
Moses was a stern and splendid king, yea, so was
    Moses. . . .
Give me more songs like David's to shake my throat
    to the pit of the belly,
And let me roll in the Isaiah thunder. . . .

Ho! the mightiest of our young men was born under
    a star in the midwinter. . . .
His name is written on the sun and it is frosted on
    the moon. . . .
Earth breathes him like an eternal spring: he is a
    second sky over the Earth.

Mighty race! mighty race!—my flesh, my flesh
Is a cup of song,
Is a well in Asia. . . .
I go about with a dark heart where the Ages sit in a
    divine thunder. . . .
My blood is cymbal-clashed and the anklets of the
    dancers tinkle there. . . .
Harp and psaltery, harp and psaltery make drunk
    my spirit. . . .

James Oppenheim

I am of the terrible people, I am of the strange
        Hebrews. . . .
Amongst the swarms fixed like the rooted stars, my
        folk is a streaming Comet,
Comet of the Asian tiger-darkness,
The Wanderer of Eternity, the eternal Wandering
        Jew. . . .

Ho! we have turned against the mightiest of our
        young men
And in that denial we have taken on the Christ,
And the two thieves beside the Christ,
And the Magdalen at the feet of the Christ,
And the Judas with thirty silver pieces selling the
        Christ,—
And our twenty centuries in Europe have the shape
        of a Cross
On which we have hung in disaster and glory. . . .

Mighty race! mighty race!—my flesh, my flesh
Is a cup of song,
Is a well in Asia.

ALFRED KREYMBORG

Alfred Kreymborg

ADAGIO: A DUET

(For J. S. and L. U.)

SHOULD you
lay ear to these lines—
you will not catch
a distant drum of hoofs,
cavalcade of Arabians,
passionate horde bearing down,
destroying your citadel—
but maybe you'll hear—
should you just
listen at the right place,
hold it tenaciously,
give your full blood to the effort—
maybe you'll note the start
of a single step,
always persistently faint,
wavering in its movement
between coming and going,
never quite arriving,
never quite passing—
and tell me which it is,
you or I
that you greet,
searching a mutual being—
and whether two aren't closer
for the labor of an ear?

Alfred Kreymborg

DIE KÜCHE

She lets the hydrant water run:
He fancies lonely, banal,
bald-headed mountains,
affected by the daily
caress of the tropical sun,
weeping tears the length of brooks
down their faces and flanks.
She lets the hydrant water run:
He hearkens Father Sebastian
cooking and spreading homely themes
over an inept-looking clavier
confounding the wits of his children
and all men's children
down to the last generation.
He marvels at the paradox,
drums his head with the tattoo:
how can a thing as small as he
shape and maintain an art
out of himself universal enough
to carry her daily vigil
to crystalled immortality?
She lets the hydrant water run.

Alfred Kreymborg

RAIN

It's all very well for you
   suddenly to withdraw
   and say, I'll come again,
but what of the bruises you've left,
what of the green and the blue,
   the yellow, purple and violet?—
don't you be telling us,
   I'm innocent of these,
   irresponsible of happenings—
didn't we see you steal next to her,
   tenderly,
   with your silver mist about you
   to hide your blandishment?—
now, what of what followed, eh?—
we saw you hover close,
   caress her,
   open her pore-cups,
   make a cross of her,
   quickly penetrate her—
she opening to you,
   engulfing you,
   every limb of her,
   bud of her, pore of her?—
don't call these things, kisses—
   mouth-kisses, hand-kisses,
   elbow, knee and toe,
and let it go at that—

Alfred Kreymborg

disappear and promise
what you'll never perform:
we've known you to slink away
    until drought-time,
    drooping-time,
    withering-time:
we've caught you crawling off
    into winter-time,
    try to cover what you've done
    with a long white scarf—
your own frozen tears
    (likely phrase!)
    and lilt your,
    I'll be back in spring!
Next spring, and you know it,
    she won't be the same,
    though she may look the same
    to you from where you are,
    and invite you down again!

Alfred Kreymborg

PEASANT

IT's the mixture of peasantry
　　makes him so slow.
He waggles his head
　　before he speaks,
like a cow
　　before she crops.
He bends to the habit
　　of dragging his feet
　　up under him,
like a measuring-worm:
　　some of his forefathers,
　　stooped over books,
　　ruled short straight lines
　　under two rows of figures
　　to keep their thin savings
　　from sifting to the floor.
Should you strike him
　　with a question,
he will blink twice or thrice
　　and roll his head about,
like an owl
　　in the pin-pricks
　　of a dawn he cannot see.
There is mighty little flesh
　　about his bones,
there is no gusto
　　in his stride:
he seems to wait

83

for the blow on the buttocks
that will drive him
another step forward—
step forward to what?
There is no land,
  no house,
  no barn,
he has ever owned;
he sits uncomfortable
  on chairs
  you might invite him to:
if you did,
  he'd keep his hat in hand
  against the moment
  when some silent pause
  for which he hearkens
  with his ear to one side
  bids him move on—
  move on where?
It doesn't matter.
He has learned
  to shrug his shoulders,
  so he'll shrug his shoulders now:
caterpillars do it
  when they're halted by a stick.
Is there a sky overhead?—
  a hope worth flying to?—
birds may know about it,
  but it's birds
  that birds descend from.

Alfred Kreymborg

BUBBLES

You had best be very cautious
    how
you say, I love you.
If you accent the I,
she has an opening for,
who are you
to strut on ahead
and hint there aren't others,
aren't, weren't and won't be?
Blurt out the love,
she has suspicion for,
    so?—
why not hitherto?—
what brings you bragging now?—
and what'll it be hereafter?
Defer to the you,
she has certitude for,
    me?
thanks, hell!—
but why argu about it?—
or fancy I'm lonesome?—
do I look as though you had to?
And having determined how
you'll say it,
you had next best ascertain
    whom
it is that you say it to.

Alfred Kreymborg

That you're sure she's the one,
that there'll never be another,
never was one before.
And having determined whom
and having learned how,
when you bring these together,
inform the far of the intimate—
like a bubble on a pond,
emerging from below,
round wonderment completed
by the first sight of the sky—
what good will it do,
if she shouldn't, I love you?—
a bubble's but a bubble once,
a bubble grows to die.

Alfred Kreymborg

DIRGE

DEATH alone
has sympathy for weariness:
understanding
of the ways
of mathematics:
of the struggle
against giving up what was given:
the plus one minus one
of nitrogen for oxygen:
and the unequal odds,
you a cell
against the universe,
a breath or two
against all time:
·Death alone
takes what is left
without protest, criticism
or a demand for more
than one can give
who can give
no more than was given:
doesn't even ask,
but accepts it as it is,
witnout examination,
valuation,
or comparison.

Alfred Kreymborg

COLOPHON

(For W. W.)

THE Occident and the Orient,
posterior and posterior,
sitting tight, holding fast
the culture dumped by them
on to primitive America,
Atlantic to Pacific,
were monumental colophons
a disorderly country fellow,
vulgar Long Islander.
not overfond of the stench
choking native respiration,
poked down off the shelf
with the aid of some
mere blades of grass;
and deliberately climbing up,
brazenly usurping one end
of the new America,
now waves his spears aloft
and shouts down valleys,
across plains,
over mountains,
into heights:
Come, what man of you
dares climb the other?

SARA TEASDALE

Sara Teasdale

WISDOM

It was a night of early spring,
  The winter-sleep was scarcely broken;
Around us shadows and the wind
  Listened for what was never spoken.

Though half a score of years are gone,
  Spring comes as sharply now as then—
But if we had it all to do
  It would be done the same again.

It was a spring that never came;
  But we have lived enough to know
That what we never have, remains;
  It is the things we have that go.

Sara Teasdale

PLACES

I

TWILIGHT

(Tucson)

ALOOF as aged kings,
Wearing like them the purple,
The mountains ring the mesa
Crowned with a dusky light;
Many a time I watched
That coming-on of darkness
Till stars burned through the heavens
Intolerably bright.

It was not long I lived there,
But I became a woman
Under those vehement stars,
For it was there I heard
For the first time my spirit
Forging an iron rule for me,
As though with slow cold hammers
Beating out word by word:

" Take love when love is given,
But never think to find it
A sure escape from sorrow
Or a complete repose;

Sara Teasdale

Only yourself can heal you,
Only yourself can lead you
Up the hard road to heaven
That ends where no one knows."

Sara Teasdale

II

FULL MOON

(Santa Barbara)

I LISTENED, there was not a sound to hear
  In the great rain of moonlight pouring down,
The eucalyptus trees were carved in silver,
  And a light mist of silver lulled the town.

I saw far off the gray Pacific bearing
  A broad white disk of flame,
And on the garden-walk a snail beside me
  Tracing in crystal the slow way he came.

Sara Teasdale

III

Winter Sun

(Lenox)

There was a bush with scarlet berries,
    And there were hemlocks heaped with snow,
With a sound like surf on long sea-beaches
    They took the wind and let it go.

The hills were shining in their samite,
    Fold after fold they flowed away;
"Let come what may," your eyes were saying,
    "At least we two have had to-day."

Sara Teasdale

IV

THERE was an evening when the sky was clear,
　　Ineffably translucent in its blue;
　　The tide was falling, and the sea withdrew
In hushed and happy music from the sheer
Shadowy granite of the cliffs; and fear
　　Of what life may be, and what death can do,
　　Fell from us like steel armor, and we knew
The beauty of the Law that holds us here.

It was as though we saw the Secret Will,
　　It was as though we floated and were free;
　　　In the south-west a planet shone serenely,
　　　And the high moon, most reticent and queenly
Seeing the earth had darkened and grown still,
　　Misted with light the meadows of the sea.

Sara Teasdale

WORDS FOR AN OLD AIR

YOUR heart is bound tightly, let
   Beauty beware;
It is not hers to set
   Free from the snare.

Tell her a bleeding hand
   Bound it and tied it;
Tell her the knot will stand
   Though she deride it.

One who withheld so long
   All that you yearned to take,
Has made a snare too strong
   For Beauty's self to break.

Sara Teasdale

THOSE WHO LOVE

THOSE who love the most
Do not talk of their love;
Francesca, Guenevere,
Dierdre, Iseult, Heloise
In the fragrant gardens of heaven
Are silent, or speak, if at all,
Of fragile, inconsequent things.

And a woman I used to know
Who loved one man from her youth,
Against the strength of the fates
Fighting in lonely pride,
Never spoke of this thing,
But hearing his name by chance,
A light would pass over her face.

Sara Teasdale

TWO SONGS FOR SOLITUDE

I

THE CRYSTAL GAZER

I SHALL gather myself into myself again,
   I shall take my scattered selves and make them
      one,
I shall fuse them into a polished crystal ball
   Where I can see the moon and the flashing sun.

I shall sit like a sibyl, hour after hour intent,
   Watching the future come and the present go—
And the little shifting pictures of people rushing
   In tiny self-importance to and fro.

Sara Teasdale

II

The Solitary

My heart has grown rich with the passing of years,
  I have less need now than when I was young
To share myself with every comer,
  Or shape my thoughts into words with my tongue.

It is one to me that they come or go
  If I have myself and the drive of my will,
And strength to climb on a summer night
  And watch the stars swarm over the hill.

Let them think I love them more than I do,
  Let them think I care, though I go alone,
If it lifts their pride, what is it to me
  Who am self-complete as a flower or a stone?

LOUIS UNTERMEYER

Louis Untermeyer

MONOLOG FROM A MATTRESS

Heinrich Heine ætat 56, loquitur:

CAN that be you, *la mouche?*   Wait till I lift
This palsied eye-lid and make sure. . . . Ah, true.
Come in, dear fly, and pardon my delay
In thus existing; I can promise you
Next time you come you'll find no dying poet—
Without sufficient spleen to see me through,
The joke becomes too tedious a jest.
I am afraid my mind is dull to-day;
I have that—something—heavier on my chest
And then, you see, I've been exchanging thoughts
With Doctor Franz.   He talked of Kant and Hegel
As though he'd nursed them both through whoop-
        ing còugh
And, as he left, he let his finger shake
Too playfully, as though to say, " Now off
With that long face—you've years and years to
        live."
I think he thinks so.   But, for Heaven's sake,
Don't credit it—and never tell Mathilde.
Poor dear, she has enough to bear already. . . .

This *was* a month!   During my lonely weeks
One person actually climbed the stairs
To seek a cripple.   It was Berlioz—
But Berlioz always was original.

Meissner was also here; he caught me unawares,
Scribbling to my old mother. " What! " he cried,
" Is the old lady of the *Dammthor* still alive?
And do you write her still? " " Each month or so."
" And is she not unhappy then, to find
How wretched you must be? " " How can she know?
You see," I laughed, " she thinks I am as well
As when she saw me last. She is too blind
To read the papers—some one else must tell
What's in my letters, merely signed by me.
Thus she is happy. For the rest—
That any son should be as sick as I,
No mother could believe."

                             Ja, so it goes.

Come here, my lotus-flower. It is best
I drop the mask to-day; the half-cracked shield
Of mockery calls for younger hands to wield.
Laugh—or I'll hug it closer to my breast.
So . . . I can be as mawkish as I choose
And give my thoughts an airing, let them loose
For one last rambling stroll before—Now look!
Why tears? You never heard me say " the end."
Before . . . before I clap them in a book
And so get rid of them once and for all.
This is their holiday—we'll let them run—
Some have escaped already. There goes one . . .
What, I have often mused, did Goethe mean?
So many years ago at Weimar, Goethe said

" Heine has all the poet's gifts but love."
Good God!   But that is all I ever had.
More than enough!   So much of love to give
That no one gave me any in return.
And so I flashed and snapped in my own fires
Until I stood, with nothing left to burn,
A twisted trunk, in chilly isolation.
Ein Fichtenbaum steht einsam—you recall?
I was that Northern tree and, in the South,
Amalia . . . So I turned to scornful cries,
Hot iron songs to save the rest of me;
Plunging the brand in my own misery.
Crouching behind my pointed wall of words,
Ramparts I built of moons and loreleys,
Enchanted roses, sphinxes, love-sick birds,
Giants, dead lads who left their graves to dance,
Fairies and phœnixes and friendly gods—
A curious frieze, half Renaissance, half Greek,
Behind which, in revulsion of romance,
I lay and laughed—and wept—till I was weak.
Words were my shelter, words my one escape,
Words were my weapons against everything.
Was I not once the son of Revolution?
Give me the lyre, I said, and let me sing
My song of battle: Words like flaming stars
Shot down with power to burn the palaces;
Words like bright javelins to fly with fierce
Hate of the oily Philistines and glide
Through all the seven heavens till they pierce
The pious hypocrites who dare to creep

Louis Untermeyer

Into the Holy Places. " Then," I cried,
" I am a fire to rend and roar and leap;
I am all joy and song, all sword and flame! "
Ha—you observe me passionate. I aim
To curb these wild emotions lest they soar
Or drive against my will. (So I have said
These many years—and still they are not tame.)
Scraps of a song keep rumbling in my head . . .
Listen—you never heard me sing before.

> When a false world betrays your trust
>   And stamps upon your fire,
> When what seemed blood is only rust,
>   Take up the lyre!

> How quickly the heroic mood
>   Responds to its own ringing;
> The scornful heart, the angry blood
>   Leap upward, singing!

Ah, that was how it used to be. But now,
Du schöner Todesengel, it is odd
How more than calm I am. Franz said it shows
Power of religion, and it does, perhaps—
Religion or morphine or poultices—God knows.
I sometimes have a sentimental lapse
And long for saviours and a physical God.
When health is all used up, when money goes,
When courage cracks and leaves a shattered will,
Then Christianity begins. For a sick Jew,
It is a very good religion . . . Still,

Louis Untermeyer

I fear that I will die as I have lived,
A long-nosed heathen playing with his scars,
A pagan killed by weltschmerz . . . I remember,
Once when I stood with Hegel at a window,
I, being full of bubbling youth and coffee,
Spoke in symbolic tropes about the stars.
Something I said about " those high
Abodes of all the blest " provoked his temper.
" Abodes?   The stars?"   He froze me with a
      sneer,
" A light eruption on the firmament."
" But," cried romantic I, " is there no sphere
Where virtue is rewarded when we die? "
And Hegel mocked, " A very pleasant whim.
So you demand a bonus since you spent
One lifetime and refrained from poisoning
Your testy grandmother! " . . . How much of
      him
Remains in me—even when I am caught
In dreams of death and immortality.

To be eternal—what a brilliant thought!
It must have been conceived and coddled first
By some old shopkeeper in Nuremberg,
His slippers warm, his children amply nursed,
Who, with his lighted meerschaum in his hand,
His nightcap on his head, one summer night
Sat drowsing at his door.   And mused, how grand
If all of this could last beyond a doubt—
This placid moon, this plump *gemüthlichkeit;*

107

Louis Untermeyer

Pipe, breath and summer never going out—
To vegetate through all eternity . . .
But no such everlastingness for me!
God, if he can, keep me from such a blight.

> *Death, it is but the long, cool night,*
> *And Life's a dull and sultry day.*
> *It darkens; I grow sleepy;*
> *I am weary of the light.*

> *Over my bed a strange tree gleams*
> *And there a nightingale is loud.*
> *She sings of love, love only . . .*
> *I hear it, even in dreams.*

My Mouche, the other day as I lay here,
Slightly propped up upon this mattress-grave
In which I've been interred these few eight years,
I saw a dog, a little pampered slave,
Running about and barking. I would have given
Heaven could I have been that dog; to thrive
Like him, so senseless—and so much alive!
And once I called myself a blithe Hellene,
Who am too much in love with life to live.
(The shrug is pure Hebraic) . . . For what I've
    been,
A lenient Lord will tax me—and forgive.
Dieu me pardonnera—c'est son metier.
But this is jesting. There are other scandals
You haven't heard . . . Can it be dusk so soon?

Louis Untermeyer

Or is this deeper darkness . . . ?   Is that you,
Mother?   How did you come?   Where are the
    candles? . . .
Over my bed a strange tree gleams—half filled
With stars and birds whose white notes glimmer
    through
Its seven branches now that all is stilled.
What?   Friday night again and all my songs
Forgotten?   Wait . . . I still can sing—
Sh'ma Yisroel Adonai Elohenu,
Adonai Echod . . .
             Mouche—Mathilde! . . .

Louis Untermeyer

WATERS OF BABYLON

WHAT presses about us here in the evening
  As you open a window and stare at a stone-gray
      sky,
And the streets give back the jangle of meaningless
      movement
  That is tired of life and almost too tired to die.

Night comes on, and even the night is wounded;
  There, on its breast, it carries a curved, white
      scar.
What will you find out there that is not torn and
      anguished?
  Can God be less distressed than the least of His
      creatures are?

Below are the blatant lights in a huddled squalor;
  Above are futile fires in freezing space.
What can they give that you should look to them
      for compassion
  Though you bare your heart and lift an imploring
      face?

They have seen, by countless waters and windows,
  The women of your race facing a stony sky;
They have heard, for thousands of years, the voices
      of women
  Asking them: " Why . . . ? "

Louis Untermeyer

Let the night be; it has neither knowledge nor pity.
One thing alone can hope to answer your fear;
It is that which struggles and blinds us and burns
      between us. . . .
  Let the night be. Close the window, belovèd.
  . . . Come here.

Louis Untermeyer

THE FLAMING CIRCLE

THOUGH for fifteen years you have chaffed me
    across the table,
  Slept in my arms and fingered my plunging heart,
I scarcely know you; we have not known each
    other.
  For all the fierce and casual contacts, something
    keeps us apart.

Are you struggling, perhaps, in a world that I see
    only dimly,
  Except as it sweeps toward the star on which I
    stand alone?
Are we swung like two planets, compelled in our
    separate orbits,
  Yet held in a flaming circle far greater than our
    own?

Last night we were single, a radiant core of com-
    pletion,
  Surrounded by flames that embraced us but left
    no burns,
To-day we are only ourselves; we have plans and
    pretensions;
  We move in dividing streets with our small and
    different concerns.

112

Louis Untermeyer

Merging and rending, we wait for the miracle. Meanwhile
   The fire runs deeper, consuming these selves in its growth.
Can this be the mystical marriage—this clash and communion;
   This pain of possession that frees and encircles us both?

Louis Untermeyer

PORTRAIT OF A MACHINE

WHAT nudity is beautiful as this
Obedient monster purring at its toil;
These naked iron muscles dripping oil
And the sure-fingered rods that never miss.
This long and shining flank of metal is
Magic that greasy labor cannot spoil;
While this vast engine that could rend the soil
Conceals its fury with a gentle hiss.

It does not vent its loathing, does not turn
Upon its makers with destroying hate.
It bears a deeper malice; lives to earn
Its master's bread and laughs to see this great
Lord of the earth, who rules but cannot learn,
Become the slave of what his slaves create.

Louis Untermeyer

ROAST LEVIATHAN

"Old Jews!" Well, David, aren't we?
What news is that to make you see so red,
To swear and almost tear your beard in half?
Jeered at? Well, let them laugh.
You can laugh longer when you're dead.

What? Are you still too blind to see?
Have you forgot your Midrash! . . . They were
        right,
The little *goyim*, with their angry stones.
You should be buried in the desert out of sight
And not a dog should howl miscarried moans
Over your foul bones. . . .

Have you forgotten what is promised us,
Because of stinking days and rotting nights?
Eternal feasting, drinking, blazing lights
With endless leisure, periods of play!
Supernal pleasures, myriads of gay
Discussions, great debates with prophet-kings!
And rings of riddling scholars all surrounding
God who sits in the very middle, expounding
The Torah. . . . *Now* your dull eyes glisten!
Listen:

It is the final Day.
A blast of Gabriel's horn has torn away

115

Louis Untermeyer

The last haze from our eyes, and we can see
Past the three hundred skies and gaze upon
The Ineffable Name engraved deep in the sun.
Now one by one, the pious and the just
Are seated by us, radiantly risen
From their dull prison in the dust.
And then the festival begins!
A sudden music spins great webs of sound
Spanning the ground, the stars and their companions;
While from the cliffs and cañons of blue air,
Prayers of all colors, cries of exultation
Rise into choruses of singing gold.
And at the height of this bright consecration,
The whole Creation's rolled before us.
The seven burning heavens unfold. . . .
We see the first (the only one we know)
Dispersed and, shining through,
The other six declining: Those that hold
The stars and moons, together with all those
Containing rain and fire and sullen weather;
Cellars of dew-fall higher than the brim;
Huge arsenals with centuries of snows;
Infinite rows of storms and swarms of seraphim. . . .

Divided now are winds and waters. Sea and land,
Tohu and Bohu, light and darkness, stand
Upright on either hand.
And down this terrible aisle,
While heaven's ranges roar aghast,
116

Louis Untermeyer

Pours a vast file of strange and hidden things:
Forbidden monsters, crocodiles with wings
And perfumed flesh that sings and glows
With more fresh colors than the rainbow knows. . . .
The *reëm*, those great beasts with eighteen horns,
Who mate but once in seventy years and die
In their own tears which flow ten stadia high.
The *shamir*, made by God on the sixth morn,
No longer than a grain of barley corn
But stronger than the bull of Bashan and so hard
It cuts through diamonds. Meshed and starred
With precious stones, there struts the shattering *ziz*
Whose groans are wrinkled thunder. . . .
For thrice three hundred years the full parade
Files past, a cavalcade of fear and wonder.
And then the vast aisle clears.

Now comes our constantly increased reward.
The Lord commands that monstrous beast,
Leviathan, to be our feast.
What cheers ascend from horde on ravenous horde!
One hears the towering creature rend the seas,
Frustrated, cowering, and his pleas ignored.
In vain his great, belated tears are poured—
For this he was created, kept and nursed.
Cries burst from all the millions that attend:
" Ascend, Leviathan, it is the end!
We hunger and we thirst! Ascend! " . . .

Observe him first, my friend.

117

Louis Untermeyer

God's deathless plaything rolls an eye
Five hundred thousand cubits high.
The smallest scale upon his tail
Could hide six dolphins and a whale.
His nostrils breathe—and on the spot
The churning waves turn seething hot.
If he be hungry, one huge fin
Drives seven thousand fishes in;
And when he drinks what he may need,
The rivers of the earth recede.
Yet he is more than huge and strong—
Twelve brilliant colors play along
His sides until, compared to him,
The naked, burning sun seems dim.
New scintillating rays extend
Through endless singing space and rise
Into an ecstasy that cries:
" Ascend, Leviathan, ascend! "

God now commands the multi-colored bands
Of angels to intrude and slay the beast
That His good sons may have a feast of food.
But as they come, Leviathan sneezes twice . . .
And, numb with sudden pangs, each arm hangs slack.
Black terror seizes them; blood freezes into ice
And every angel flees from the attack!
God, with a look that spells eternal law,
Compels them back.
But, though they fight and smite him tail and jaw,
Nothing avails; upon his scales their swords
118

Break like frayed cords or, like a blade of straw,
Bend towards the hilt and wilt like faded grass.
Defeat and fresh retreat. . . . But once again
God's murmurs pass among them and they mass
With firmer steps upon the crowded plain.
Vast clouds of spears and stones rise from the
    ground;
But every dart flies past and rocks rebound
To the disheartened angels falling around.

A pause.
The angel host withdraws
With empty boasts throughout its sullen files.
Suddenly God smiles. . . .
On the walls of heaven a tumble of light is caught.
Low thunder rumbles like an afterthought;
And God's slow laughter calls:
" Behemot!·"

> *Behemot, sweating blood,*
> *Uses for his daily food*
> *All the fodder, flesh and juice*
> *That twelve tall mountains can produce.*
>
> *Jordan, flooded to the brim,*
> *Is a single gulp to him;*
> *Two great streams from Paradise*
> *Cool his lips and scarce suffice.*
>
> *When he shifts from side to side*
> *Earthquakes gape and open wide;*

Louis Untermeyer

When a nightmare makes him snore,
All the dead volcanoes roar.

In the space between each toe,
Kingdoms rise and saviours go;
Epochs fall and causes die
In the lifting of his eye.

Wars and justice, love and death,
These are but his wasted breath;
Chews a planet for his cud—
Behemot sweating blood.

Roused from his unconcern,
Behemot burns with anger.
Dripping sleep and languor from his heavy haunches,
He turns from deep disdain and launches
Himself upon the thickening air,
And, with weird cries of sickening despair,
Flies at Leviathan.
None can surmise the struggle that ensues—
The eyes lose sight of it and words refuse
To tell the story in its gory might.
Night passes after night,
And still the fight continues, still the sparks
Fly from the iron sinews, . . . till the marks
Of fire and belching thunder fill the dark
And, almost torn asunder, one falls stark,
Hammering upon the other! . . .
What clamor now is born, what crashings rise!
Hot lightnings lash the skies and frightening cries
120

Louis Untermeyer

Clash with the hymns of saints and seraphim.
The bloody limbs thrash through a ruddy dusk,
Till one great tusk of Behemot has gored
Leviathan, restored to his full strength,
Who, dealing fiercer blows in those last throes,
Closes on reeling Behemot at length—
Piercing him with steel-pointed claws,
Straight through the jaws to his disjointed head.
And both lie dead.

Then come the angels!
With hoists and levers, joists and poles,
With knives and cleavers, ropes and saws,
Down the long slopes to the gaping maws,
The angels hasten; hacking and carving,
So nought will be lacking for the starving
Chosen of God, who in frozen wonderment
Realize now what the terrible thunder meant.
How their mouths water while they are looking
At miles of slaughter and sniffing the cooking!
Whiffs of delectable fragrance swim by;
Spice-laden vagrants that float and entice,
Tickling the throat and brimming the eye.
Ah! what rejoicing and crackling and roasting!
Ah! How the boys sing as, cackling and boasting,
The angels' old wives and their nervous assistants
Run in to serve us. . . .

And while we are toasting
The Fairest of All, they call from the distance—

Louis Untermeyer

The rare ones of Time, they share our enjoyment;
Their only employment to bear jars of wine
And shine like the stars in a circle of glory.
Here sways Rebekah accompanied by Zilpah;
Miriam plays to the singing of Bilhah;
Hagar has tales for us, Judith her story;
Esther exhales bright romances and musk.
There, in the dusky light, Salome dances.
Sara and Rachel and Leah and Ruth,
Fairer than ever and all in their youth,
Come at our call and go by our leave.
And, from her bower of beauty, walks Eve
While, with the voice of a flower, she sings
Of Eden, young earth and the birth of all things. . . .

Peace without end.
Peace will descend on us, discord will cease;
And we, now so wretched, will lie stretched out
Free of old doubt, on our cushions of ease.
And, like a gold canopy over our bed,
The skin of Leviathan, tail-tip to head,
Soon will be spread till it covers the skies.
Light will still rise from it; millions of bright
Facets of brilliance, shaming the white
Glass of the moon, inflaming the night.

So Time shall pass and rest and pass again,
Burn with an endless zest and then return,
Walk at our side and tide us to new joys;

Louis Untermeyer

God's voice to guide us, beauty as our staff.
Thus shall Life be when Death has disappeared. . . .

Jeered at?   Well, let them laugh.

JOHN GOULD FLETCHER

John Gould Fletcher

A REBEL

Tie a bandage over his eyes,
And at his feet
Let rifles drearily patter
Their death-prayers of defeat.

Throw a blanket over his body,
It need no longer stir;
Truth will but stand the stronger
For all who died for her.

Now he has broken through
To his own secret place;
Which, if we dared to do,
We would have no more power left to look
    on that dead face.

John Gould Fletcher

THE ROCK

THIS rock, too, was a word;
A word of flame and force when that which hurled
The stars into their places in the night
First stirred.

And, in the summer's heat,
Lay not your hand on it, for while the iron hours
        beat
Gray anvils in the sky, it glows again
With unfulfilled desire.

Touch it not; let it stand
Ragged, forlorn, still looking at the land;
The dry blue chaos of mountains in the distance,
The slender blades of grass it shelters are
Its own dark thoughts of what is near and far.
Your thoughts are yours, too; naked let them stand.

John Gould Fletcher

BLUE WATER

SEA-VIOLINS are playing on the sands;
Curved bows of blue and white are flying over the
pebbles,
See them attack the chords—dark basses, glinting
trebles.
Dimly and faint they croon, blue violins.
" Suffer without regret," they seem to cry,
" Though dark your suffering is, it may be music,
Waves of blue heat that wash midsummer sky;
Sea-violins that play along the sands."

John Gould Fletcher

PRAYERS FOR WIND

LET the winds come,
And bury our feet in the sands of seven deserts;
Let strong breezes rise,
Washing our ears with the far-off sounds of the foam.
Let there be between our faces
Green turf and a branch or two of back-tossed trees;
Set firmly over questioning hearts
The deep unquenchable answer of the wind.

John Gould Fletcher

IMPROMPTU

My mind is a puddle in the street reflecting green
    Sirius;
In thick dark groves trees huddle lifting their
    branches like beckoning hands.
We eat the grain, the grain is death, all goes back
    to the earth's dark mass,
All but a song which moves across the plain like the
    wind's deep-muttering breath.
Bowed down upon the earth, man sets his plants and
    watches for the seed,
Though he be part of the tragic pageant of the sky,
    no heaven will aid his mortal need.
I find flame in the dust, a word once uttered that will
    stir again,
And a wine-cup reflecting Sirius in the water held
    in my hands.

John Gould Fletcher

CHINESE POET AMONG BARBARIANS

THE rain drives, drives endlessly,
Heavy threads of rain;
The wind beats at the shutters,
The surf drums on the shore;
Drunken telegraph poles lean sideways;
Dank summer cottages gloom hopelessly;
Bleak factory-chimneys are etched on the filmy dis-
      tance,
Tepid with rain.
It seems I have lived for a hundred years
Among these things;
And it is useless for me now to make complaint
      against them.
For I know I shall never escape from this dull bar-
      barian country,
Where there is none now left to lift a cool jade
      winecup,
Or share with me a single human thought.

John Gould Fletcher

SNOWY MOUNTAINS

HIGHER and still more high,
Palaces made for cloud,
Above the dingy city-roofs
Blue-white like angels with broad wings,
Pillars of the sky at rest
The mountains from the great plateau
Uprise.

But the world heeds them not;
They have been here now for too long a time.
The world makes war on them,
Tunnels their granite cliffs,
Splits down their shining sides,
Plasters their cliffs with soap-advertisements,
Destroys the lonely fragments of their peace.

Vaster and still more vast,
Peak after peak, pile after pile,
Wilderness still untamed,
To which the future is as was the past,
Barrier spread by Gods,
Sunning their shining foreheads,
Barrier broken down by those who do not need
The joy of time-resisting storm-worn stone,
The mountains swing along
The south horizon of the sky;
Welcoming with wide floors of blue-green ice
The mists that dance and drive before the sun.

133

John Gould Fletcher

THE FUTURE

AFTER ten thousand centuries have gone,
Man will ascend the last long pass to know
That all the summits which he saw at dawn
Are buried deep in everlasting snow.

Below him endless gloomy valleys, chill,
Will wreathe and whirl with fighting cloud, driven
  by the wind's fierce breath;
But on the summit, wind and cloud are still:—
Only the sunlight, and death.

And staggering up to the brink of the gulf man will
  look down
And painfully strive with weak sight to explore
The silent gulfs below which the long shadows
  drown;
Through every one of these he passed before.

Then since he has no further heights to climb,
And naught to witness he has come this endless way,
On the wind-bitten ice cap he will wait for the last
  of time,
And watch the crimson sunrays fading of the world's
  latest day:

And blazing stars will burst upon him there,
Dumb in the midnight of his hope and pain,
Speeding no answer back to his last prayer,
And, if akin to him, akin in vain.

John Gould Fletcher

UPON THE HILL

A HUNDRED miles of landscape spread before me
    like a fan;
Hills behind naked hills, bronze light of evening on
    them shed;
How many thousand ages have these summits spied
    on man?
How many thousand times shall I look on them ere
    this fire in me is dead?

John Gould Fletcher

THE ENDURING

If the autumn ended
Ere the birds flew southward,
If in the cold with weary throats
They vainly strove to sing,
Winter would be eternal;
Leaf and bush and blossom
Would never once more riot
In the spring.

If remembrance ended
When life and love are gathered,
If the world were not living
Long after one is gone,
Song would not ring, nor sorrow
Stand at the door in evening;
Life would vanish and slacken,
Men would be changed to stone.

But there will be autumn's bounty
Dropping upon our weariness,
There will be hopes unspoken
And joys to haunt us still;
There will be dawn and sunset
Though we have cast the world away,
And the leaves dancing
Over the hill.

JEAN STARR UNTERMEYER

Jean Starr Untermeyer

OLD MAN

WHEN an old man walks with lowered head
And eyes that do not seem to see,
I wonder does he ponder on
The worm he was or is to be.

Or has he turned his gaze within,
Lost to his own vicinity;
Erecting in a doubtful dream
Frail bridges to Infinity.

Jean Starr Untermeyer

TONE PICTURE

(Malipiero: *Impressioni Dal Vero*)

Across the hot square, where the barbaric sun
Pours coarse laughter on the crowds,
Trumpets throw their loud nooses
From corner to corner.
Elephants, whose indifferent backs
Heave with red lambrequins,
Tigers with golden muzzles,
Negresses, greased and turbaned in green and yellow,
Weave and interweave in the merciless glare of noon.
The sun flicks here and there like a throned tyrant,
Snapping his whip.
From amber platters, the smells ascend
Of overripe peaches mingled with dust and heated
        oils.
Pages in purple run madly about,
Rolling their eyes and grinning with huge, fright-
        ened mouths.

And from a high window—a square of black velvet—
A haughty figure stands back in the shadow,
Aloof and silent.

Jean Starr Untermeyer

THEY SAY—

THEY say I have a constant heart, who know
    Not anything of how it turns and yields
    First here, first there; nor how in separate fields
It runs to reap and then remains to sow;
How, with quick worship, it will bend and glow
    Before a line of song, an antique vase,
    Evening at sea; or in a well-loved face
Seek and find all that Beauty can bestow.

Yet they do well who name it with a name,
    For all its rash surrenders call it true.
Though many lamps be lit, yet flame is flame;
    The sun can show the way, a candle too.
The tribute to each fragment is the same
    Service to all of Beauty—and her due.

Jean Starr Untermeyer

RESCUE

WIND and wave and the swinging rope
Were calling me last night;
None to save and little hope,
No inner light.

Each snarling lash of the stormy sea
Curled like a hungry tongue.
One desperate splash—and no use to me
The noose that swung!

Death reached out three crooked claws
To still my clamoring pain.
I wheeled about, and Life's gray jaws
Grinned once again.

To sea I gazed, and then I turned
Stricken toward the shore,
Praying half-crazed to a moon that burned
Above your door.

And at your door, you discovered me;
And at your heart, I sobbed . . .
And if there be more of eternity
Let me be robbed.

144

Jean Starr Untermeyer

Let me be clipped of that heritage
And burned for ages through;
Freed and stripped of my fear and rage—
But not of you.

Jean Starr Untermeyer

MATER IN EXTREMIS

I STAND between them and the outer winds,
But I am a crumbling wall.
They told me they could bear the blast alone,
They told me: that was all.
But I must wedge myself between
Them and the first snowfall.

Riddled am I by onslaughts and attacks
I thought I could forestall;
I reared and braced myself to shelter them
Before I heard them call.
I cry them, God, a better shield!
I am about to fall.

Jean Starr Untermeyer

SELF-REJECTED

PLOW not nor plant this arid mound.
Here is no sap for seed,
No ferment for your need—
Ungrateful ground!

No sun can warm this spot
God has forgot;
No rain can penetrate
Its barren slate.

Demonic winds blow last year's stubble
From its hard slope.
Go, leave the hopeless without hope;
Spare your trouble.

H. D.

H. D.

HOLY SATYR

Most holy Satyr,
like a goat,
with horns and hooves
to match thy coat
of russet brown,
I make leaf-circlets
and a crown of honey-flowers
for thy throat;
where the amber petals
drip to ivory,
I cut and slip
each stiffened petal
in the rift
of carven petal:
honey horn
has wed the bright
virgin petal of the white
flower cluster: lip to lip
let them whisper,
let them lilt, quivering:

Most holy Satyr,
like a goat,
hear this our song,
accept our leaves,
love-offering,
return our hymn;

151

H. D.

like echo fling
a sweet song,
answering note for note.

H. D.

LAIS

LET her who walks in Paphos
take the glass,
let Paphos take the mirror
and the work of frosted fruit,
gold apples set
with silver apple-leaf,
white leaf of silver
wrought with vein of gilt.

Let Paphos lift the mirror;
let her look
into the polished center of the disk.

Let Paphos take the mirror:
did she press
flowerlet of flame-flower
to the lustrous white
of the white forehead?
did the dark veins beat
a deeper purple
than the wine-deep tint
of the dark flower?

Did she deck black hair,
one evening, with the winter-white
flower of the winter-berry?
Did she look (reft of her lover)

H. D.

at a face gone white
under the chaplet
of white virgin-breath?

Lais, exultant, tyrannizing Greece,
Lais who kept her lovers in the porch,
lover on lover waiting
(but to creep
where the robe brushed the threshold
where still sleeps Lais),
so she creeps, Lais,
to lay her mirror at the feet
of her who reigns in Paphos.

Lais has left her mirror,
for she sees no longer in its depth
the Lais' self
that laughed exultant,
tyrannizing Greece.

Lais has left her mirror,
for she weeps no longer,
finding in its depth
a face, but other
than dark flame and white
feature of perfect marble.

Lais has left her mirror
(so one wrote)
to her who reigns in Paphos;

H. D.

Lais who laughed a tyrant over Greece,
Lais who turned the lovers from the porch,
that swarm for whom now
Lais has no use;
Lais is now no lover of the glass,
seeing no more the face as once it was,
wishing to see that face and finding this.

H. D.

HELIODORA

HE and I sought together,
over the spattered table,
rhymes and flowers,
gifts for a name.

He said, among others,
I will bring
(and the phrase was just and good,
but not as good as mine)
" the narcissus that loves the rain."

We strove for a name,
while the light of the lamps burnt thin
and the outer dawn came in,
a ghost, the last at the feast
or the first,
to sit within
with the two that remained
to quibble in flowers and verse
over a girl's name.

He said, " the rain loving,"
I said, " the narcissus, drunk,
drunk with the rain."

Yet I had lost
for he said,

H. D.

" the rose, the lover's gift,
is loved of love,"
he said it,
" loved of love;"
I waited, even as he spoke,
to see the room filled with a light,
as when in winter
the embers catch in a wind
when a room is dank:
so it would be filled, I thought,
our room with a light
when he said
(and he said it first)
" the rose, the lover's delight,
is loved of love,"
but the light was the same.

Then he caught,
seeing the fire in my eyes,
my fire, my fever, perhaps,
for he leaned
with the purple wine
stained in his sleeve,
and said this:
" Did you ever think
a girl's mouth
caught in a kiss
is a lily that laughs? "

I had not.
I saw it now

H. D.

as men must see it forever afterwards;
no poet could write again,
" the red-lily,
a girl's laugh caught in a kiss;"
it was his to pour in the vat
from which all poets dip and quaff,
for poets are brothers in this.

So I saw the fire in his eyes,
it was almost my fire
(he was younger)
I saw the face so white;
my heart beat,
it was almost my phrase,
I said, " surprise the muses,
take them by surprise;
it is late,
rather it is dawn-rise,
those ladies sleep, the nine,
our own king's mistresses."

A name to rhyme,
flowers to bring to a name,
what was one girl faint and shy,
with eyes like the myrtle
(I said: " her underlids
are rather like myrtle"),
to vie with the nine?

Let him take the name,
he had the rhymes,

H. D.

" the rose, loved of love,"
" the lily, a mouth that laughs,"
he had the gift,
" the scented crocus,
the purple hyacinth,"
what was one girl to the nine?

He said:
" I will make her a wreath;"
he said:
" I will write it thus:
' *I will bring you the lily that laughs,*
I will twine
with soft narcissus, the myrtle,
sweet crocus, white violet,
the purple hyacinth and, last,
the rose, loved of love,
that these may drip on your hair
the less soft flowers,
may mingle sweet with the sweet
of Heliodora's locks,
myrrh-curled.' "

(He wrote myrrh-curled,
I think, the first.)

I said:
" they sleep, the nine,"
when he shouted swift and passionate:
" *that* for the nine!
Above the mountains

H. D.

the sun is about to wake,
and to-day white violets
shine beside white lilies
adrift on the mountain side;
to-day the narcissus opens
that loves the rain."

I watched him to the door,
catching his robe
as the wine-bowl crashed to the floor,
spilling a few wet lees
(ah, his purple hyacinth!);
I saw him out of the door,
I thought:
there will never be a poet,
in all the centuries after this,
who will dare write,
after my friend's verse,
" a girl's mouth
is a lily kissed."

H. D.

TOWARD THE PIRÆUS

Slay with your eyes, Greek,
men over the face of the earth,
slay with your eyes, the host,
puny, passionless, weak.

Break, as the ranks of steel
broke of the Persian host:
craven, we hated them then:
now we would count them Gods
beside these, spawn of the earth.

Grant us your mantle, Greek;
grant us but one
to fright (as your eyes) with a sword,
men, craven and weak,
grant us but one to strike
one blow for you, passionate Greek.

H. D.

I

You would have broken my wings,
but the very fact that you knew
I had wings, set some seal
on my bitter heart, my heart
broke and fluttered and sang.

You would have snared me,
and scattered the strands of my nest;
but the very fact that you saw,
sheltered me, claimed me,
set me apart from the rest

Of men—of *men* made you a god,
and me, claimed me, set me apart
and the song in my breast, yours, yours forever—
if I escape your evil heart.

H. D.

II

I LOVED you:
men have writ and women have said
they loved,
but as the Pythoness stands by the altar,
intense and may not move,

till the fumes pass over;
and may not falter nor break,
till the priest has caught the words
that mar or make
a deme or a ravaged town;

so I, though my knees tremble,
my heart break,
must note the rumbling,
heed only the shuddering
down in the fissure beneath the rock
of the temple floor;

must wait and watch
and may not turn nor move,
nor break from my trance to speak
so slight, so sweet,
so simple a word as love.

H. D.

III

WHAT had you done
had you been true,
I can not think,
I may not know.

What could we do
were I not wise,
what play invent,
what joy devise?

What could we do
if you were great?
(Yet were you lost,
who were there, then,
to circumvent
the tricks of men?)

What can we do,
for curious lies
have filled your heart,
and in my eyes
sorrow has writ
that I am wise.

H. D.

IV

If I had been a boy,
I would have worshiped your grace,
I would have flung my worship
before your feet,
I would have followed apart,
glad, rent with an ecstasy
to watch you turn
your great head, set on the throat,
thick, dark with its sinews,
burned and wrought
like the olive stalk,
and the noble chin
and the throat.

I would have stood,
and watched and watched
and burned,
and when in the night,
from the many hosts, your slaves,
and warriors and serving men
you had turned
to the purple couch and the flame
of the woman, tall like cypress tree
that flames sudden and swift and free
as with crackle of golden resin
and cones and the locks flung free
like the cypress limbs,

H. D.

bound, caught and shaken and loosed,
bound, caught and riven and bound
and loosened again,
as in rain of a kingly storm
or wind full from a desert plain.

So, when you had risen
from all the lethargy of love and its heat,
you would have summoned me, me alone,
and found my hands,
beyond all the hands in the world,
cold, cold, cold,
intolerably cold and sweet.

H. D.

V

IT was not chastity that made me cold nor fear,
only I knew that you, like myself, were sick
of the puny race that crawls and quibbles and lisps
of love and love and lovers and love's deceit.

It was not chastity that made me wild but fear
that my weapon, tempered in different heat,
was over-matched by yours, and your hand
skilled to yield death-blows, might break

With the slightest turn—no ill-will meant—
my own lesser, yet still somewhat fine-wrought
fiery-tempered, delicate, over-passionate steel.

CONRAD AIKEN

Conrad Aiken

SEVEN TWILIGHTS

I

THE ragged pilgrim, on the road to nowhere,
Waits at the granite milestone. It grows dark.
Willows lean by the water. Pleas of water
Cry through the trees. And on the boles and boughs
Green water-lights make rings, already paling.
Leaves speak everywhere. The willow leaves
Silverly stir on the breath of moving water,
Birch-leaves, beyond them, twinkle, and there on the
     hill,
And the hills beyond again, and the highest hill,
Serrated pines, in the dusk, grow almost black.
By the eighth milestone on the road to nowhere
He drops his sack, and lights once more the pipe
There often lighted. In the dusk-sharpened sky
A pair of night-hawks windily sweep, or fall,
Booming, toward the trees. Thus had it been
Last year, and the year before, and many years:
Ever the same. "Thus turns the human track
Backward upon itself, I stand once more
By this small stream . . ." Now the rich sound
     of leaves,
Turning in air to sway their heavy boughs,
Burns in his heart, sings in his veins, as spring
Flowers in veins of trees; bringing such peace
As comes to seamen when they dream of seas.

171

Conrad Aiken

" O trees! exquisite dancers in gray twilight!
Witches! fairies! elves! who wait for the moon
To thrust her golden horn, like a golden snail,
Above that mountain—arch your green benediction
Once more over my heart. Muffle the sound of bells,
Mournfully human, that cries from the darkening
        valley;
Close, with your leaves, about the sound of water:
Take me among your hearts as you take the mist
Among your boughs!" . . . Now by the granite
        milestone,
On the ancient human road that winds to nowhere,
The pilgrim listens, as the night air brings
The murmured echo, perpetual, from the gorge
Of barren rock far down the valley. Now, ·
Though twilight here, it may be starlight there;
Mist makes elfin lakes in the hollow fields;
The dark wood stands in the mist like a somber
        island
With one red star above it. . . . " This I should
        see,
Should I go on, follow the falling road,—
This I have often seen. . . . But I shall stay
Here, where the ancient milestone, like a watchman,
Lifts up its figure eight, its one gray knowledge,
Into the twilight; as a watchman lifts
A lantern, which he does not know is out."

Conrad Aiken

II

Now by the wall of the ancient town I lean
Myself, like ancient wall and dust and sky,
And the purple dusk, grown old, grown old in heart.
Shadows of clouds flow inward from the sea.
The mottled fields grow dark. The golden wall
Grows gray again, turns stone again, the tower,
No longer kindled, darkens against a cloud.
Old is the world, old as the world am I;
The cries of sheep rise upward from the fields,
Forlorn and strange; and wake an ancient echo
In fields my heart has known, but has not seen.
" These fields "—an unknown voice beyond the wall
Murmurs—" were once the province of the sea.
Where now the sheep graze, mermaids were at play,
Sea-horses galloped, and the great jeweled tortoise
Walked slowly, looking upward at the waves,
Bearing upon his back a thousand barnacles,
A white acropolis . . ." The ancient tower
Sends out, above the houses and the trees,
And the wide fields below the ancient walls,
A measured phrase of bells. And in the silence
I hear a woman's voice make answer then:
" Well, they are green, although no ship can sail
        them. . . .
Sky-larks rest in the grass, and start up singing
Before the girl who stoops to pick sea-poppies.
Spiny, the poppies are, and oh how yellow!

173

Conrad Aiken

And the brown clay is runneled by the rain. . . ."
A moment since, the sheep that crop the grass
Had long blue shadows, and the grass-tips sparkled:
Now all grows old. . . . O voices strangely speaking,
Voices of man and woman, voices of bells,
Diversely making comment on our time
Which flows and bears us with it into dusk,
Repeat the things you say! Repeat them slowly
Upon this air, make them an incantation
For ancient tower, old wall, the purple twilight,
This dust, and me. But all I hear is silence,
And something that may be leaves or may be sea.

Conrad Aiken

III

When the tree bares, the music of it changes:
Hard and keen is the sound, long and mournful;
Pale are the poplar boughs in the evening light
Above my house, against a slate-cold cloud.
When the house ages and the tenants leave it,
Cricket sings in the tall grass by the threshold;
Spider, by the cold mantel, hangs his web.
Here, in a hundred years from that clear season
When first I came here, bearing lights and music,
To this old ghostly house my ghost will come,—
Pause in the half-light, turn by the poplar, glide
Above tall grasses through the broken door.
Who will say that he saw—or the dusk deceived
        him—
A mist with hands of mist blow down from the tree
And open the door and enter and close it after?
Who will say that he saw, as midnight struck
Its tremulous golden twelve, a light in the window,
And first heard music, as of an old piano,
Music remote, as if it came from the earth,
Far down; and then, in the quiet, eager voices?
". . . Houses grow old and die, houses have ghosts—
Once in a hundred years we return, old house,
And live once more." . . . And then the ancient
        answer,
In a voice not human, but more like creak of boards

Conrad Aiken

Or rattle of panes in the wind—" Not as the owner,
But as a guest you come, to fires not lit
By hands of yours. . . . Through these long-silent
        chambers
Move slowly, turn, return, and bring once more
Your lights and music. It will be good to talk."

Conrad Aiken

IV

" This is the hour," she said, " of transmutation:
It is the eucharist of the evening, changing
All things to beauty. Now the ancient river,
That all day under the arch was polished jade,
Becomes the ghost of a river, thinly gleaming
Under a silver cloud. . . . It is not water:
It is that azure stream in which the stars
Bathe at the daybreak, and become immortal. . . ."
" And the moon," said I—not thus to be outdone—
" What of the moon?   Over the dusty plane-trees
Which crouch in the dusk above their feeble lanterns,
Each coldly lighted by his tiny faith;
The moon, the waxen moon, now almost full,
Creeps whitely up. . . . Westward the waves of
          cloud,
Vermilion, crimson, violet, stream on the air,
Shatter to golden flakes in the icy green
Translucency of twilight. . . . And the moon
Drinks up their light, and as they fade or darken,
Brightens. . . . O monstrous miracle of the twilight,
That one should live because the others die! "
" Strange too," she answered, " that upon this azure
Pale-gleaming ghostly stream, impalpable—
So faint, so fine that scarcely it bears up
The petals that the lantern strews upon it,—
These great black barges float like apparitions,
Loom in the silver of it, beat upon it,

Moving upon it as dragons move on air."
" Thus always," then I answered,—looking never
Toward her face, so beautiful and strange
It grew, with feeding on the evening light,—
" The gross is given, by inscrutable God,
Power to beat wide wings upon the subtle.
Thus we ourselves, so fleshly, fallible, mortal,
Stand here, for all our foolishness, transfigured:
Hung over nothing in an arch of light
While one more evening like a wave of silence
Gathers the stars together and goes out."

Conrad Aiken

V

Now the great wheel of darkness and low clouds
Whirs and whirls in the heavens with dipping rim;
Against the ice-white wall of light in the west
Skeleton trees bow down in a stream of air.
Leaves, black leaves and smoke, are blown on the
       wind;
Mount upward past my window; swoop again;
In a sharp silence, loudly, loudly falls
The first cold drop, striking a shriveled leaf. . . .
Doom and dusk for the earth! Upward I reach
To draw chill curtains and shut out the dark,
Pausing an instant, with uplifted hand,
To watch, between black ruined portals of cloud,
One star,—the tottering portals fall and crush it.
Here are a thousand books! here is the wisdom
Alembicked out of dust, or out of nothing;
Choose now the weightiest word, most golden page,
Most somberly musicked line; hold up these lan-
       terns,—
These paltry lanterns, wisdoms, philosophies,—
Above your eyes, against this wall of darkness;
And you'll see—what? One hanging strand of cob-
       web,
A window-sill a half-inch deep in dust . . .
Speak out, old wise-men! Now, if ever, we need you.
Cry loudly, lift shrill voices like magicians
Against this baleful dusk, this wail of rain. . . .

Conrad Aiken

But you are nothing! Your pages turn to water
Under my fingers: cold, cold and gleaming,
Arrowy in the darkness, rippling, dripping—
All things are rain. . . . Myself, this lighted room,
What are we but a murmurous pool of rain? . . .
The slow arpeggios of it, liquid, sibilant,
Thrill and thrill in the dark. World-deep I lie
Under a sky of rain. Thus lies the sea-shell
Under the rustling twilight of the sea;
No gods remember it, no understanding
Cleaves the long darkness with a sword of light.

Conrad Aiken

VI

Heaven, you say, will be a field in April,
A friendly field, a long green wave of earth,
With one domed cloud above it. There you'll lie
In noon's delight, with bees to flash above you,
Drown amid buttercups that blaze in the wind,
Forgetting all save beauty. There you'll see
With sun-filled eyes your one great dome of cloud
Adding fantastic towers and spires of light,
Ascending, like a ghost, to melt in the blue.
Heaven enough, in truth, if you were there!
Could I be with you I would choose your noon,
Drown amid buttercups, laugh with the intimate
        grass,
Dream there forever. . . . But, being older, sadder,
Having not you, nor aught save thought of you,
It is not spring I'll choose, but fading summer;
Not noon I'll choose, but the charmed hour of dusk.
Poppies? A few! And a moon almost as red. . . .
But most I'll choose that subtler dusk that comes
Into the mind—into the heart, you say—
When, as we look bewildered at lovely things,
Striving to give their loveliness a name,
They are forgotten; and other things, remembered,
Flower in the heart with the fragrance we call grief.

Conrad Aiken

VII

In the long silence of the sea, the seaman
Strikes twice his bell of bronze.   The short note
    wavers
And loses itself in the blue realm of water.
One sea-gull, paired with a shadow, wheels, wheels;
Circles the lonely ship by wave and trough;
Lets down his feet, strikes at the breaking water,
Draws up his golden feet, beats wings, and rises
Over the mast. . . . Light from a crimson cloud
Crimsons the sluggishly creeping foams of waves;
The seaman, poised in the bow, rises and falls
As the deep forefoot finds a way through waves;
And there below him, steadily gazing westward,
Facing the wind, the sunset, the long cloud,
The goddess of the ship, proud figurehead,
Smiles inscrutably, plunges to crying waters,
Emerges streaming, gleaming, with jewels falling
Fierily from carved wings and golden breasts;
Steadily glides a moment, then swoops again.
Carved by the hand of man, grieved by the wind;
Worn by the tumult of all the tragic seas,
Yet smiling still, unchanging, smiling still
Inscrutably, with calm eyes and golden brow—
What is it that she sees and follows always,
Beyond the molten and ruined west, beyond
The light-rimmed sea, the sky itself?   What secret
Gives wisdom to her purpose?   Now the cloud
182

Conrad Aiken

In final conflagration pales and crumbles
Into the darkening waters. Now the stars
Burn softly through the dusk. The seaman strikes
His small lost bell again, watching the west
As she below him watches. . . . O pale goddess
Whom not the darkness, even, or rain or storm,
Changes; whose great wings are bright with foam,
Whose breasts are cold as the sea, whose eyes for-
     ever
Inscrutably take that light whereon they look—
Speak to us!   Make us certain, as you are,
That somewhere, beyond wave and wave and wave,
That dreamed-of harbor lies which we would find.

Conrad Aiken

TETÉLESTAI

I

How shall we praise the magnificence of the dead,
The great man humbled, the haughty brought to
    dust?
Is there a horn we should not blow as proudly
For the meanest of us all, who creeps his days,
Guarding his heart from blows, to die obscurely?
I am no king, have laid no kingdoms waste,
Taken no princes captive, led no triumphs
Of weeping women through long walls of trumpets;
Say rather I am no one, or an atom;
Say rather, two great gods in a vault of starlight
Play ponderingly at chess; and at the game's end
One of the pieces, shaken, falls to the floor
And runs to the darkest corner; and that piece
Forgotten there, left motionless, is I. . . .
Say that I have no name, no gifts, no power,
Am only one of millions, mostly silent;
One who came with lips and hands and a heart,
Looked on beauty, and loved it, and then left it.
Say that the fates of time and space obscured me,
Led me a thousand ways to pain, bemused me,
Wrapped me in ugliness; and like great spiders
Dispatched me at their leisure. . . . Well, what
    then?

Should I not hear, as I lie down in dust,
The horns of glory blowing above my burial?

II

Morning and evening opened and closed above me:
Houses were built above me; trees let fall
Yellowing leaves upon me, hands of ghosts,
Rain has showered its arrows of silver upon me
Seeking my heart; winds have roared and tossed me;
Music in long blue waves of sound has borne me
A helpless weed to shores of unthought silence;
Time, above me, within me, crashed its gongs
Of terrible warning, sifting the dust of death;
And here I lie. Blow now your horns of glory
Harshly over my flesh, you trees, you waters!
You stars and suns, Canopus, Deneb, Rigel,
Let me, as I lie down, here in this dust,
Hear, far off, your whispered salutation!
Roar now above my decaying flesh, you winds,
Whirl out your earth-scents over this body, tell me
Of ferns and stagnant pools, wild roses, hillsides!
Anoint me, rain, let crash your silver arrows
On this hard flesh! I am the one who named you,
I lived in you, and now I die in you.
I, your son, your daughter, treader of music,
Lie broken, conquered. . . . Let me not fall in
    silence.

Conrad Aiken

III

I, the restless one; the circler of circles;
Herdsman and roper of stars, who could not capture
The secret of self; I who was tyrant to weaklings,
Striker of children; destroyer of women; corrupter
Of innocent dreamers, and laugher at beauty; I,
Too easily brought to tears and weakness by music,
Baffled and broken by love, the helpless beholder
Of the war in my heart of desire with desire, the
    struggle
Of hatred with love, terror with hunger; I
Who laughed without knowing the cause of my
    laughter, who grew
Without wishing to grow, a servant to my own body;
Loved without reason the laughter and flesh of a
    woman,
Enduring such torments to find her! I who at last
Grow weaker, struggle more feebly, relent in my
    purpose,
Choose for my triumph an easier end, look backward
At earlier conquests; or, caught in the web, cry out
In a sudden and empty despair, " Tetélestai! "
Pity me, now! I, who was arrogant, beg you!
Tell me, as I lie down, that I was courageous.
Blow horns of victory now, as I reel and am van-
    quished.
Shatter the sky with trumpets above my grave.

Conrad Aiken

IV

. . . Look! this flesh how it crumbles to dust and
    is blown!
These bones, how they grind in the granite of frost
    and are nothing!
This skull, how it yawns for a flicker of time in the
    darkness
Yet laughs not and sees not! It is crushed by a
    hammer of sunlight,
And the hands are destroyed. . . . Press down
    through the leaves of the jasmine,
Dig through the interlaced roots—nevermore will
    you find me;
I was no better than dust, yet you cannot replace
    me. . . .
Take the soft dust in your hand—does it stir: does
    it sing?
Has it lips and a heart? Does it open its eyes to
    the sun?
Does it run, does it dream, does it burn with a
    secret, or tremble
In terror of death? Or ache with tremendous de-
    cisions? . . .
Listen! . . . It says: "I lean by the river. The
    willows
Are yellowed with bud. White clouds roar up from
    the south

And darken the ripples; but they cannot darken
    my heart,
Nor the face like a star in my heart! . . . Rain
    falls on the water
And pelts it, and rings it with silver. The willow
    trees glisten,
The sparrows chirp under the eaves; but the face
    in my heart
Is a secret of music. . . . I wait in the rain and
    am silent."
Listen again! . . . It says: " I have worked, I am
    tired,
The pencil dulls in my hand: I see through the
    window
Walls upon walls of windows with faces behind them,
Smoke floating up to the sky, an ascension of sea-
    gulls.
I am tired. I have struggled in vain, my decision
    was fruitless,
Why then do I wait? with darkness, so easy, at
    hand! . . .
But to-morrow, perhaps. . . . I will wait and en-
    dure till to-morrow! . . ."
Or again: " It is dark. The decision is made. I
    am vanquished
By terror of life. The walls mount slowly about me
In coldness. I had not the courage. I was for-
    saken.
I cried out, was answered by silence. . . . Tetéles-
    tai! . . ."

Conrad Aiken

V

Hear how it babbles!—Blow the dust out of your
    hand,
With its voices and visions, tread on it, forget it,
    turn homeward
With dreams in your brain. . . . This, then, is the
    humble, the nameless,—
The lover, the husband and father, the struggler
    with shadows,
The one who went down under shoutings of chaos!
    The weakling
Who cried his " forsaken! " like Christ on the dark-
    ening hilltop! . . .
This, then, is the one who implores, as he dwindles
    to silence,
A fanfare of glory. . . . And which of us dares to
    deny him!

EDNA ST. VINCENT MILLAY

Edna St. Vincent Millay

EIGHT SONNETS

I

WHEN you, that at this moment are to me
Dearer than words on paper, shall depart,
And be no more the warder of my heart,
Whereof again myself shall hold the key;
And be no more, what now you seem to be,
The sun, from which all excellencies start
In a round nimbus, nor a broken dart
Of moonlight, even, splintered on the sea;

I shall remember only of this hour—
And weep somewhat, as now you see me weep—
The pathos of your love, that, like a flower,
Fearful of death yet amorous of sleep,
Droops for a moment and beholds, dismayed,
The wind whereon its petals shall be laid.

Edna St. Vincent Millay

II

What's this of death, from you who never will die?
Think you the wrist that fashioned you in clay,
The thumb that set the hollow just that way
In your full throat and lidded the long eye
So roundly from the forehead, will let lie
Broken, forgotten, under foot some day
Your unimpeachable body, and so slay
The work he most had been remembered by?

I tell you this: whatever of dust to dust
Goes down, whatever of ashes may return
To its essential self in its own season,
Loveliness such as yours will not be lost,
But, cast in bronze upon his very urn,
Make known him Master, and for what good reason.

Edna St. Vincent Millay

III

I know I am but summer to your heart,
And not the full four seasons of the year;
And you must welcome from another part
Such noble moods as are not mine, my dear.
No gracious weight of golden fruits to sell
Have I, nor any wise and wintry thing;
And I have loved you all too long and well
To carry still the high sweet breast of spring.

Wherefore I say: O love, as summer goes,
I must be gone, steal forth with silent drums,
That you may hail anew the bird and rose
When I come back to you, as summer comes.
Else will you seek, at some not distant time,
Even your summer in another clime.

Edna St. Vincent Millay

IV

Here is a wound that never will heal, I know,
Being wrought not of a dearness and a death
But of a love turned ashes and the breath
Gone out of beauty; never again will grow
The grass on that scarred acre, though I sow
Young seed there yearly and the sky bequeath
Its friendly weathers down, far underneath
Shall be such bitterness of an old woe.

That April should be shattered by a gust,
That August should be leveled by a rain,
I can endure, and that the lifted dust .
Of man should settle to the earth again;
But that a dream can die, will be a thrust
Between my ribs forever of hot pain.

Edna St. Vincent Millay

V

What lips my lips have kissed, and where, and why,
I have forgotten, and what arms have lain
Under my head till morning; but the rain
Is full of ghosts to-night, that tap and sigh
Upon the glass and listen for reply;
And in my heart there stirs a quiet pain,
For unremembered lads that not again
Will turn to me at midnight with a cry.

Thus in the winter stands the lonely tree,
Nor knows what birds have vanished one by one,
Yet knows its boughs more silent than before:
I cannot say what loves have come and gone;
I only know that summer sang in me
A little while, that in me sings no more.

Edna St. Vincent Millay

VI

Euclid alone has looked on Beauty bare.
Let all who prate of Beauty hold their peace,
And lay them prone upon the earth and cease
To ponder on themselves, the while they stare
At nothing, intricately drawn nowhere
In shapes of shifting lineage; let geese
Gabble and hiss, but heroes seek release
From dusty bondage into luminous air.

O blinding hour, O holy, terrible day,
When first the shaft into his vision shone
Of light anatomized!   Euclid alone
Has looked on Beauty bare.   Fortunate they
Who, though once only and then but far away,
Have heard her massive sandal set on stone.

Edna St. Vincent Millay

VII

Oh, oh, you will be sorry for that word!
Give back my book and take my kiss instead.
Was it my enemy or my friend I heard?—
" What a big book for such a little head! "
Come, I will show you now my newest hat,
And you may watch me purse my mouth and prink.
Oh, I shall love you still and all of that.
I never again shall tell you what I think.

I shall be sweet and crafty, soft and sly;
You will not catch me reading any more;
I shall be called a wife to pattern by;
And some day when you knock and push the door,
Some sane day, not too bright and not too stormy,
I shall be gone, and you may whistle for me.

Edna St. Vincent Millay

VIII

Say what you will, and scratch my heart to find
The roots of last year's roses in my breast;
I am as surely riper in my mind
As if the fruit stood in the stalls confessed.
Laugh at the unshed leaf, say what you will,
Call me in all things what I was before,
A flutterer in the wind, a woman still;
I tell you I am what I was and more.

My branches weigh me down, frost cleans the air,
My sky is black with small birds bearing south;
Say what you will, confuse me with fine care,
Put by my word as but an April truth,—
Autumn is no less on me that a rose
Hugs the brown bough and sighs before it goes.

BIBLIOGRAPHY

BIBLIOGRAPHY

(The following lists include poetical works only)

AMY LOWELL

A Dome of Many-Colored Glass	Houghton Mifflin Co.	1912
Sword Blades and Poppy Seed	The Macmillan Company	1914
Men, Women and Ghosts	The Macmillan Company	1916
Can Grande's Castle	The Macmillan Company	1918
Pictures of the Floating World	The Macmillan Company	1919
Legends	Houghton Mifflin Co.	1921
Fir-Flower Tablets	Houghton Mifflin Co.	1921

ROBERT FROST

A Boy's Will	Henry Holt and Company	1914
North of Boston	Henry Holt and Company	1915
Mountain Interval	Henry Holt and Company	1916

CARL SANDBURG

Chicago Poems	Henry Holt and Company	1916
Cornhuskers	Henry Holt and Company	1918
Smoke and Steel	Harcourt, Brace and Co.	1920
Slabs of the Sunburnt West	Harcourt, Brace and Co.	1922

VACHEL LINDSAY

Rhymes to be Traded for Bread	Privately Printed; Springfield, Ill.	1912
General William Booth Enters Into Heaven	Mitchell Kennerley	1913
The Congo and Other Poems	The Macmillan Company	1915
The Chinese Nightingale	The Macmillan Company	1917
The Golden Whales of California	The Macmillan Company	1920

Bibliography

JAMES OPPENHEIM

Monday Morning and Other Poems	Sturgis & Walton Co.	1909
Songs for the New Age	The Century Company	1914
War and Laughter	The Century Company	1915
The Book of Self	Alfred A. Knopf	1917
The Solitary	B. W. Huebsch	1919
The Mystic Warrior	Alfred A. Knopf	1921

ALFRED KREYMBORG

Mushrooms	Alfred A. Knopf	1916
Plays for Poem-Mimes	The Others Press	1918
Plays for Merry Andrews	The Sunwise Turn	1920
Blood of Things	Nicholas L. Brown	1921

SARA TEASDALE

Sonnets to Duse	The Poet Lore Co.	1907
Helen of Troy	G. P. Putnam's Sons	1911
Rivers to the Sea	The Macmillan Company	1915
Love Songs	The Macmillan Company	1917
Flame and Shadow	The Macmillan Company	1920

LOUIS UNTERMEYER

The Younger Quire	Moods Publishing Co.	1911
First Love	Sherman French & Co.	1911
Challenge	The Century Company	1914
" — and Other Poets "	Henry Holt and Company	1916
The Poems of Heinrich Heine	Henry Holt and Company	1917
These Times	Henry Holt and Company	1917
Including Horace	Harcourt, Brace and Co.	1919
The New Adam	Harcourt, Brace and Co.	1920
Heavens	Harcourt, Brace and Co.	1922

JOHN GOULD FLETCHER

Fire and Wine	Grant Richards (London)	1913
The Dominant City	Max Goschen (London)	1913
Fool's Gold	Max Goschen (London)	1913
The Book of Nature	Constable & Co. (London)	1913
Visions of the Evening	Erskine Macdonald (London)	1913
Irradiations	Houghton Mifflin Co.	1915
Goblins and Pagodas	Houghton Mifflin Co.	1916
Japanese Prints	The Four Seas Company	1918
The Tree of Life	The Macmillan Company	1919
Breakers and Granite	The Macmillan Company	1921

Bibliography

JEAN STARR UNTERMEYER
  Growing Pains   B. W. Huebsch   1918
  Dreams Out of Darkness B. W. Huebsch   1921

H. D.
  Sea Garden   Houghton Mifflin Co.   1916
  Hymen   Henry Holt and Co.   1921

CONRAD AIKEN
  Earth Triumphant   The Macmillan Company 1914
  Turns and Movies   Houghton Mifflin Co.   1916
  The Jig of Forslin   The Four Seas Company 1916
  Nocturne of Remembered
    Spring   The Four Seas Company 1917
  The Charnel Rose   The Four Seas Company 1918
  The House of Dust   The Four Seas Company 1920
  Punch: the Immortal Liar Alfred A. Knopf   1921

EDNA ST. VINCENT MILLAY
  Renascence   Mitchell Kennerley   1917
  A Few Figs from Thistles Frank Shay   1920
  The Lamp and the Bell Frank Shay   1921
  Aria Da Capo   Mitchell Kennerley   1921
  Second April   Mitchell Kennerley   1921